The IEA Health and Welfare Unit

Choice in Welfare No. 32

Stakeholder Welfare

Frank Field

With Commentaries by

Pete Alcock
Alan Deacon (Editor)
David G. Green
Melanie Phillips

IEA Health and Welfare Unit
London, 1996

First published November 1996

The IEA Health and Welfare Unit
2 Lord North St
London SW1P 3LB

ISBN 0-255 36390-7
ISSN 1362-9565

Front cover graphics from CorelDraw 6.

Typeset by the IEA Health and Welfare Unit
in New Century Schoolbook 10 on 11 point
Printed in Great Britain by
St Edmundsbury Press Ltd
Blenheim Industrial Park, Newmarket Road
Bury St Edmunds, Suffolk

Contents

Foreword

In common with some other publications in the Choice in Welfare Series, the purpose of *Stakeholder Welfare* is to make available in an accessible format the main points of view on a given issue. This collection is designed especially for students of social science in universities and sixth forms.

The main essay has been produced by Frank Field MP, for many years one of the most productive and insightful thinkers about social policy reform. His essay is followed by critiques from four different vantage points: self-interest, character, civil society, and the common good.

In addition to contributing one of the critiques, Professor Alan Deacon also acted as editor to ensure that the collection was properly balanced for use in teaching.

David G. Green
Series Editor

The Authors

Frank Field has been the Labour Member of Parliament for Birkenhead since 1979. He has been a front-bench spokesman on education and social security, chairman of the Commons Social Services Select Committee and is currently the chairman of the Social Security Select Committee. Recent publications include: *Losing Out: the Emergence of Britain's Underclass*, and *An Agenda for Britain*.

Other Institute of Community Studies publications allied to *How To Pay For the Future* are: Field, F., *Making Welfare Work*, 1995 (out of print); Field, F., Halligan, L. and Owen, M., *Europe Isn't Working*, 1994; and Field, F. and Owen, M., *Beyond Punishment: Hard Choices on the Road to Full Employability*, 1994.

Pete Alcock is Professor of Social Policy at Sheffield Hallam University. He has written widely in the area of poverty, social security and anti-poverty policy and is the author of *Understanding Poverty* and *Social Poverty in Britain*. His major research interests are in the field of local anti-poverty action and welfare rights. Professor Alcock is currently the Chair of the Social Policy Association, and he is a member of the Editorial Boards of *Journal of Social Policy* and *Benefits*.

Alan Deacon is Professor of Social Policy and Dean of Economic Social Studies and Law at the University of Leeds. He edited the *Journal of Social Policy* between 1987 and 1991. He has written extensively on the history of social policy, unemployment and the problems of single homeless people. His books include *Reserved for the Poor*, with Jonathan Bradshaw, 1983 and *Roads to Resettlement*, with Jill Vincent and Robert Walker, 1995.

Dr David Green is the Director of the Health and Welfare Unit at the Institute of Economic Affairs. His books include *The Welfare State: For Rich or for Poor?*, 1982; *The New Right: The Counter Revolution in Political, Economic and Social Thought*, 1987; *Equalizing People*, 1990; *Reinventing Civil Society*, 1993; and *Community Without Politics*, 1996. His work has also been published in journals such as the *Journal of Social Policy*, *Political Quarterly*, *Philosophy of the Social Sciences* and *Policy and Politics*.

Melanie Phillips is a columnist for *The Observer* who writes about social issues and political culture. She is the author of a controversial new book, *All Must Have Prizes* (Little Brown) which charts the disastrous effects of our culture of individualism upon the education system and the moral order.

Editorial Introduction

Alan Deacon

The revolution of thought involved in this new policy is far larger than dwellers in the present day can easily realise unless they are skilful at recapturing their own past moods.

THIS was how *The Economist* magazine described the White Paper on *Employment Policy* which was published by the wartime Coalition Government in June 1944.[1] The 'revolution in thought' to which it referred was the acceptance that the maintenance of a high and stable level of employment would be one of the 'primary aims and responsibilities' of post-war governments. A similarly important change in thinking has taken place in recent years, but this time the shift has been in Labour Party policy towards the Welfare State.

The New Welfare Debate

This 'revolution in thought' regarding welfare has not occurred in isolation. It has been part of a fundamental reappraisal of social and economic policy following the election of Tony Blair as Leader in 1994. Central to the so-called 'Blair revolution' has been the adoption of policies towards public ownership, the levels of personal taxation and public spending, and the responsibilities and obligations of individuals which appear to have more in common with the Thatcher governments of the 1980s than with earlier Labour administrations. Indeed, one of the paradoxes of British politics in the 1990s is that, as Thatcherism seems to be on the wane as a political force, so some of the ideas most closely associated with it appear to be being adopted by the other parties.

In no area of policy is this more evident than it is in social security. Labour, for example, has proposed a 'welfare to work' scheme which incorporates an element of compulsion which would have been unthinkable a few years ago.[2] Similarly, it has abandoned its commitment to uprate national insurance pensions in line with earnings and envisages a much greater role for private pensions. Perhaps most strikingly of all, the shadow spokesman on social security, Chris Smith, claimed in June 1996 that a Labour government would save over £1 billion a year through a vigorous campaign to counter benefit fraud. Such has been the speed and scale of the changes in Labour thinking that much of the academic literature now has a somewhat dated air. What are still described as 'New Right' writers or ideas no longer seem very new or particularly right wing.[3] This is not, of course, to suggest that the changes have gone unchallenged. Indeed, the most interesting—and fierce—debates about welfare are now to be found on the centre/left and left.

The sources of Labour's new agenda have been much discussed, and particular attention has been paid to the influences upon Tony Blair himself. Prominent amongst these are his long-standing commitment to Christian Socialism and his recent interest in the Communitarian ideas developed by Amitai Etzioni and others in the United States. A further and more immediate influence is the work of a disparate group of journalists, academics and politicians recently labelled 'Blair's Gurus'.[4] In the case of social policy the most significant of these 'gurus' is Frank Field.

Frank Field

Frank Field has been Labour MP for Birkenhead since 1979, and before that was Director of the Child Poverty Action Group and founder of the Low Pay Unit. He has always been a free thinker, reluctant to accept the constraints of party discipline. In the 1970s, for example, he was amongst the first to advocate the sale of council houses, and in the 1990s he has proposed radical changes in both pensions policy and in provision for the unemployed. In *Private Pensions for All*, he argued that the existing State Earnings Related Pension Scheme (SERPS) should be abandoned and that every employee and self employed person should be compelled to join a private pensions scheme. In *Beyond Punishment*, he called for a major expansion of training and job creation programmes but also for far more stringent checks upon those suspected of not looking for work or of 'working and signing'.[5]

This iconoclasm has made him 'many conservatives' favourite Labour politician'[6] but in the past has distanced him from the mainstream of Labour thinking. The election of Tony Blair, however, has increased Field's influence, while his role as Chair of the House of Commons Social Security Committee has been highly significant. It is the reports of the Social Security Committee on benefit fraud, for example, which have done more than anything else to create a near consensus between the parties over an issue which until recently was generally regarded as the province of the far right and the tabloid press.[7]

Many of Field's earlier proposals are incorporated in *Making Welfare Work*, which was published in 1995 and is his most important book to date. In *Making Welfare Work* Field builds upon his earlier ideas to develop a powerful critique both of current welfare provision and of the anti-poverty strategies pursued by parties of the centre-left since the Second World War. It is this critique which is first summarised and then extended further in his essay in this volume.

Field's starting point in *Making Welfare Work* is the growth of means testing. The impact of this change, he argues, 'has been so profound that it is difficult to overestimate its importance'.[8] The increase in means-tested benefits has been a disaster because of the way in which the rules which determine entitlement to such benefits influence the behaviour and the character of those who claim them. It is inevitable that means tests exclude from benefit those who have saved, or who work part-time, or whose partner is in employment. In so doing they penalise the very activities and attributes which a welfare system should foster. They 'actively undermine the moral fabric of our characters'.

The answer is to remodel the benefit system such that it harnesses the self-interest of individuals and works with and not against the grain of human nature. The way to do this is to extend the scope of contributory insurance. Insurance benefits are paid irrespective of the means of claimants and their partners and provide a platform from which they can move away from dependence on benefits, as well as offering fewer opportunities for fraud and deception.

Such a shift away from means tests and towards an insurance-based system would be costly, and would encounter two immediate problems. First it would be at the expense of increases in the level of the existing means-tested benefits, and so would do nothing to increase the income of those who are currently poor. Field's response is that this is the price which has to be paid for reducing the scope of means testing. In any case, he argues, policies which have focused upon the poor have failed in the past and are very unlikely to be more successful at the present time when voters seem even more reluctant to accept higher levels of personal taxation. The second immediate problem is that an insurance strategy has to find ways of persuading people to spread their income more evenly over their lifetime; contributing enough when in work to fund their retirement and to provide cover against unemployment, illness or disability. This, Field argues, will not be possible if voters suspect that their contributions are being used to finance benefits for other people. It is here that his concept of 'Stakeholder Welfare' is crucial.

Stakeholder Welfare

'Stakeholding' has become an increasingly fashionable term in British political debates, although there is scant agreement about what the term actually means. Some industrialists have used it to advocate the expansion of employee share-ownership schemes which they see as a way of increasing the involvement and identification of workers' with the firms which employ them. Economists such as Hutton have gone on to argue that such a shift in the ownership of private industry is essential to counter the 'short termism' engendered by city institutions.[9] Politicians have referred more generally to a 'Stakeholder Society' which is character-ised by a much greater sense of inclusiveness and mutual responsibility and in which few are unable to participate because of unemployment or homelessness

Field's use of the term, however, is quite specific. For him the defining characteristic of 'Stakeholder Welfare' is that people own the welfare capital created by their contributions and those of their employers. This, he argues, is essential if welfare is to reflect the growing emphasis upon autonomy in contemporary industrial societies; 'individuals increasingly want to decide matters themselves.' The importance which people attach to autonomy is exemplified by the way in which the membership of personal pension schemes has soared despite the adverse publicity they have received. The reason, he suggests, is that people are attracted by the idea of owning directly the capital created by their savings. The pension is perceived as personal property. It will be paid out of an identifiable fund to which the recipient has contributed and is not vulnerable to changes in public policy. This is in stark contrast to SERPS, under which the pensions paid in any one year are funded by the contributions and taxes paid that year. Politicians have chopped and changed the rules and significantly reduced entitlements. 'There can be few more certain worse buys at the current time', says Field, and anyone persuaded otherwise should 'be made a ward of court'. The obvious lesson from this is to abandon schemes such as SERPS in favour to those which combine 'compulsory membership with personal ownership of the welfare capital which results'. In other words, to move to 'Stakeholder Welfare'.

Such a move will have two important consequences. First, contributors will have to be assured that they will receive the benefits they have paid for, and this precludes redistribution within the scheme from the better-off contributors to the less well-off. It will still be possible for governments to pay contributions on behalf of those who would otherwise be excluded—indeed it will be essential that they do. The cost of these contributions, however, will be met out of general taxation, it will not fall on the other contributors. The second consequence will be the need for new 'Stakeholder Corporations' to administer the insurance-based schemes. These will have to be representative of all those contributing to the fund—including the government—but will be autonomous agencies. The model is the mutual aid bodies of the nineteenth century—collectivism without the state.

The Commentaries

The central themes of Field's analysis are discussed and debated in the four commentaries included in this text and in his response to them. Pete Alcock questions Field's assumptions regarding the lack of political support for redistribution and argues that the crisis of welfare identified by Field can only be met through a more comprehensive strategy which encompasses economic as well as social policy. To be effective such a strategy must be more egalitarian in its aims and incorporate a much greater role for the state in the planning of investment and the regulation of the labour market.

My own commentary welcomes Field's emphasis upon the links between benefits and behaviour, but challenges his discussion of character and human nature. I argue that the language employed by Field is too redolent of individualist explanations of poverty, and that there is a danger that this will distract from the significance of his critique of means tests.

Melanie Phillips applauds the moral basis of Field's arguments and his attempt to restore the question of moral character to the forefront of welfare debates. Nevertheless, she expresses a number of reservations about the viability of his proposals, and is particularly sceptical about the autonomous corporations which Field proposes should administer the insurance schemes.

David Green welcomes what he sees as Field's challenge to socialist determinism. He argues, however, that Field is wrong to focus on means tests and that the insurance benefits proposed by Field will be just as vulnerable to malingering. More generally, Green questions whether the incentives created by the benefit system are as important as Field suggests because different people react in different ways to the same incentives. From Green's perspective, Field is still underestimating the importance of character. Similarly, Green believes that Field's autonomous corporations will prove to be a chimera because the effect of compulsory insurance will be to crowd out the voluntary agencies which are the only true basis of a functioning civil society.

It will be obvious that the authors of the four commentaries write from different perspectives. All are critical of Field to a greater or lesser extent, but they share a belief in the importance of the debate and the significance of Field's contribution to it.

Notes

1   Ministry of Reconstruction, *Employment Policy*, Cmd 6527 1944. *The Economist*, 3 June 1944.

2   *Getting Welfare to Work : A New Vision for Social Security*, Labour Party Policy Document, June 1996. For the background to much New Labour thinking see Mandelson, P. and Liddle, R., *The Blair Revolution: Can New Labour Deliver?*, London: Faber and Faber, 1996.

3   A good example is the otherwise excellent collection, George, V. and Page, R. (eds.), *Modern Thinkers on Welfare*, Hemel Hempstead: Harvester Wheatsheaf. The 'New Right' is represented by Hayek and Friedman, economists whose most important works were published in 1960 and 1962 respectively.

4   Willets, D., *Blair's Gurus*, London: Centre For Policy Studies, 1996.

5   Field, F. and Owen, M., *Private Pensions For All*, London: Fabian Society, 1993; Field, F. and Owen, M., *Beyond Punishment: Hard Choices on the Road to Full Employability*, London: Institute of Community Studies, 1994.

6   Willets, D., *op. cit.*, p. 31.

7   House of Commons Social Security Committee, Session 1994-95, Fifth Report, *The Work of the Department of Social Security and its Agencies*, HC 382; Session 1995-96, Third Report, *Housing Benefit Fraud*, HC 90-91.

8   Field, F., *Making Welfare Work: Reconstructing Welfare for the Millennium*, London: Institute of Community Studies, 1995.

9   Hutton, W., *The State We're In*, London: Jonathan Cape, 1994.

Making Welfare Work:
The Underlying Principles

Frank Field

The High Politics of Welfare

THE importance of welfare in the political debate has varied dramatically over the last two centuries. The early Victorian political settlement, coming as it did with the repeal of the Corn Laws and the passing of the Bank Charter Act, took most commercial and monetary questions out of party debate. The implementation of the new Poor Law similarly settled social policy.

This consensus was overturned largely by the efforts of Joseph Chamberlain. His 'unauthorised programme' doubly holed the status quo below the water line. The Peelite view that Opposition should not put forward a programme until it had been 'called in' was directly confronted. Following hard on the heels of this challenge came another Chamberlain broadside. Fiscal policy ceased to be a matter of raising the necessary revenue with the minimum disturbance to private interest. Redistribution entered into the political fray. Welfare was again set on a course for high politics.

The Chamberlain challenge was one which Gladstone appeared only too anxious to counter, but his opposition brought devastating electoral consequences for the old Liberal party. A new welfare settlement had to await the Liberal landslide of 1906, and the use to which Lloyd George and Churchill put this overwhelming majority. New Liberalism's attempt to forge a sustaining coalition of voters again marked a new high-water mark in the politics of welfare.

Welfare is set once again to become *the* issue of high politics. A new political settlement is falling into place over the political landscape. The collapse of the Berlin Wall and the cross-party agreement on the priority given to controlling inflation have largely removed foreign affairs and the running of the economy from the day-to-day battle of party politics. Welfare is sucked into the centre of this political vacuum.

Welfare would have eventually taken that premier position anyway as the post-war settlement breaks up. The pressures fracturing the old welfare consensus come from a budget which:

- appears out of control;
- undermines good government;
- is increasingly destructive of honesty, effort, savings and thereby of self-improvement.

Each of these political pressures is considered in Section II. Yet even without such forces pushing welfare higher up the political agenda, the issue enters the major political league for a distinctly different reason. The self-imposed political innocence of the post-war political settlement, with its unspoken assumption of welfare's neutrality on character, now looks incredibly naïve.

The largest single item in welfare's budget is pensions. Most of the budget therefore goes to individuals who have earned their entitlement, the payment of which has wholly beneficial effects. This is not true, however, of all of the welfare budget, and it is particularly not so of the fastest growing area of welfare—that of means-tested assistance. It is this part of the budget which goes largely to claimants of working age. Means tests are the cancer within the welfare state, rotting decent values and overwhelming the honesty and dignity of recipients in almost equal proportions.

That welfare affects behaviour is not of concern only to recipients. It throws down an immediate challenge to would-be reformers. The age when contributors to the debate on reforming welfare can do so dispassionately, without detailing the values they wish to promote through welfare reform, should be brought to a swift end.

The beliefs and objectives underpinning *Making Welfare Work* and the follow up volume, *How To Pay For The Future*, are sevenfold:

- Welfare influences behaviour by the simple device of bestowing rewards (benefits) and allotting punishments (loss of benefits). With a third of central Government expenditure allocated by welfare, payments on this scale play an important part on setting down the general ground rules for society's behaviour. The nature of our character depends in part on the values which welfare fosters.

- Welfare should aim to maximise self-improvement, without which all is lost. Work, effort, savings and honesty must all be rewarded rather than, as so often at present, being penalised by welfare's provisions.

- Welfare has to reflect the pivotal role which self-interest plays within our motivations. Satisfying self-interest in ways which promote the common good should be a major objective of welfare policy.

- Welfare has to work with the changing labour market, giving people incentives and support to maximise their opportunities and thereby their rewards from work.

- Welfare should openly reward good behaviour and it should be used to enhance those roles which the country values. Those individuals who wish to buck the system and oppose the verities of civilised life should not be encouraged.

- Welfare should be given a central role guaranteeing universal citizenship in an age of stakeholder democracy.

- The aim of welfare's reconstruction therefore is to hold fast to the inclusiveness which was the central objective of post-war reforms, by offering new institutions popularly owned and controlled by the membership, which will win the enthusiasm of the majority.

These ideas, and a programme transforming today's welfare state, were put forward in *Making Welfare Work*. This paper revisits the ideas laid out in *Making Welfare Work* and sets out how these ideas can be taken forward. *Making Welfare Work* is now out of print. However, a fuller argument for the next stage of *Making Welfare Work*'s argument will appear in *How To Pay For The Future*. This will include data from the Government Actuary's Department on the costings of the proposed reforms.

The Centre Cannot Hold[1]

Key Political Assumptions

*M*AKING *Welfare Work* was based on five central political assumptions. The first was that the current welfare status quo cannot hold. Indeed, the surprise is that it has held for so long. In the current arrangements the poor are treated as inferior beings pushed increasingly onto means-tested assistance. Here lies the second political assumption. The disengagement from state welfare will continue with the poor being made increasingly vulnerable to second-class status. Only by seizing the initiative, by developing and offering a new welfare settlement which appeals strongly to the vast majority, might it be possible to secure for the poor full membership of the new welfare settlement.

The third assumption underscores the belief that welfare does not operate in a social vacuum. It influences character for good or ill. Because of the growing dominance of means tests, welfare increasingly acts destructively, penalising effort, attacking savings and taxing honesty. The traditional cry that means tests stigmatise is now a minor issue. They do for some, but this is simply no longer the main issue. Means tests are steadily recruiting a nation of cheats and liars. Hence the urgency for reform. The responsibility for this appalling state of affairs rests primarily with politicians who support the existence and extension of means-tested welfare.

But, fourthly, any new settlement will be dominated by the emerging values which prize ownership and control. What I have called the growing social autonomy of voters—wishing to do 'their own thing' determined on a basis of free association—will be the touchstone of the new welfare. The old-style corporatism of the state-run system either lies dead in the water, or awaits that fate. The futility of trying to resurrect the old order is the fifth political assumption which underpins *Making Welfare Work*.

1. A Pro-poor Campaign

Social surveys have played a pivotal role in shaping Britain's social policy. At the turn of the century the 'condition of the people' was the issue—although it was dressed in a number of different disguises. The results of a whole series of social surveys came to dominate this debate: how many were poor; how best to help them?

Seebohm Rowntree was a key player in establishing who was poor. Rowntree defined poverty in such a way as to include the majority of the working-class. The food component of Rowntree's calculations was by far and away the largest element in his poverty budget. The single observer to realise the full implication of what Rowntree had done was the statistician A.L. Bowley. As early as 1915 he observed: 'the food ration used by Mr Rowntree as a minimum is more liberal... than that obtained by the majority of the working-class even in Europe in 1913, and by the great majority of the unskilled and agricultural labourers in England before the end of the fall of prices in 1895... it has come as a surprise to many people to learn what a large proportion of even an advanced population is insufficiently fed ... and that the poor and the working-class were really interchangeable terms in past generations'.[2] Working-class politics and programmes to help the poor naturally overlapped. Tackling poverty appealed to a huge constituency.

Bowley's comments referred to times past. While the interchangeability of the poor with much of the working-class was still true at the time Bowley wrote, it became less so in the inter-war years. Steadily rising living standards for those in work was a marked feature of the 1920s and 1930s. It was those out of work who were set apart. In contrast, the post-war period of full employment ensured a steadily rising living standard for all those who wished to take work, which was plentifully available.

As the post-war boom faltered, and before the much more serious unemployment patterns of the 1970s and 1980s became what appear to be a permanent feature in the industrial landscape, a group of individuals, largely outside the labour market, was left untouched by the general increase in living standards. A new age dawned. The poor, as a group, were no longer identical with the working-class, but were becoming distinctly separate as differences in living standards cut them off from the mainstream of working-class families. Hence the start of Britain's anti-poverty programme which targeted help on the poor only.

I do not believe there is public support for continuing a programme aimed only at eradicating poverty. Moreover, even if there were such a coalition in the making, I would argue against its mobilisation. Anti-poverty strategies until now have not merely failed, but have actually entrenched the poor even more firmly within their ghettos.

Here was the starting point of *Making Welfare Work*. Could a raft of policies be produced which the majority of the electorate would back with such enthusiasm that its comprehensiveness—of including the poor in the good life—would also be bought?

The aim was that this enthusiasm would spring from:

- building a welfare reconstruction which was imbued with the aspirations and values of the majority;
- a programme offering to counter, as far as human action could, the vagaries of economic and social life;
- turning on its head the approach from one of being done good to to one of carving out one's own well being.

2. Growth in Expenditure

There are other changes already affecting Britain which will ensure a remaking of welfare's compact. A number of mighty forces are beginning to draw up and aim their fire-power against the social security budget. Change will be forced on a number of fronts. First there is the impact of the sheer size and growth of the social security budget, from 23 per cent of government expenditure in 1979 to 31 per cent in 1996. Matching that growth has been its share of GDP; from 9 per cent in 1979 to almost 13 per cent by 1996.

No matter how it is measured, the social security budget is growing at an extraordinary rate. The Government has abandoned its aspiration to cut the budget in real terms. It now embraces only the more modest goal of limiting social security expenditure's advance to below the underlying growth rate in the economy. The current claims by the Secretary of State to have reduced the annual growth and set it on a path below the underlying growth rate of the economy must be set against his own record, let alone that of the whole Government since 1979. During the period of Peter Lilley's stewardship the social security budget has each year burst through the annual increase agreed for it by the Cabinet in its annual public expenditure round by at least £1 billion and usually by £3 billion.

3. The Undermining of Good Government

An attack on the social security budget has also opened up on a second front. Its inexorable growth is preventing good government. Since 1992-3 public expenditure has grown by £43 billion. Of this increase, the social security programme, which already claimed the largest share of the total budget, cornered the lion's share of the increase, or two-fifths of the total rise in Government spending. In other words the largest budget is growing faster than any of the other major areas of public expenditure. The sheer size and the apparent uncontrollability of the largest of public budgets makes it increasingly difficult for the Government to prioritise expenditure over the range of its total programme. Aneurin Bevan once claimed that socialism is the language of priorities. They are certainly the basis of good government. Over the past 17 years in particular, cabinet ministers have been taken prisoner by the imperial guard at the DSS whose overspend increasingly limits the ability of other ministers to take independent action.

4. More for Less

The third force challenging the rise of social security expenditure stems from nothing less than a double paradox. Over wide tracts of public expenditure the Government has introduced market-orientated reforms. Their aim was not only to gain better value for money, but for those gains to cover the cost of any likely increase in demand for services. But, as

Nicholas Bosanquet argues in his Social Market Foundation publication, *Public Spending into the Millennium*,[3] the impact of the reforms has been such, and the performance of parts of the public sector so enhanced, that the reforms themselves have created new swathes of demand. The reforms have therefore had the opposite effect to what the Government intended.

The second, and associated, paradox concerns how any increase in the supply of public goods can be paid for. Whether or not it is a true reflection, practically all senior politicians believe that to suggest a generalised rise in direct taxation would court electoral disaster. Apart from printing money or borrowing, moves which would be immediately punished by the international capital markets, only indirect taxation is available for such financing. Here, then, is the second and linked paradox. Demands for an increase in public expenditure are most easily voiced by middle-class groups, those with sharp elbows, anxious to get themselves and their families to the top of the queue. The most expedient political way of paying for those increases is by indirect taxation which bears most heavily on poorer people. Increases in public expenditure paid for by poorer groups but disproportionately benefiting richer groups is hardly a strategy a future radical government can contemplate with ease.

5. Tory Means-Test Strategy

At the heart of this Government's strategy to control social security expenditure is a grotesque misunderstanding of welfare's dynamics; herein lies the fourth force which has already begun destroying the beliefs which underpin the post-war welfare settlement. Tory Governments since 1979 have made the targeting of benefits the major means by which growth in the social security budget is controlled. That targeting has overwhelmingly assumed the form of means testing. The Government's view is that these benefits provide the final safety-net in the welfare state. The reduction or abolition of insurance benefits saves money and anyone then left without adequate resources of their own will be eligible for means-tested assistance.

The post-war welfare settlement envisaged that means tests would have a place in the new scheme of things, but their role was only ever meant to be a residual one. The intention was that as individuals became eligible for national insurance benefits the numbers claiming means-tested benefits would fall.

The opposite has occurred. There are three main classes of benefits. The cost of contributory benefits since 1979 has increased by less than 30 per cent. Expenditure on non-means-tested and non-contributory benefits has risen by a little over 100 per cent. Expenditure on means-tested welfare, however, has rocketed, by almost 300 per cent in 16 years, i.e. ten times more than the increased expenditure in insurance benefits.

Table 1
Percentage increases in benefit expenditure
between 1978/9 and 1994/5

1	contributory benefits	28.5
2	non-contributory benefits	105.1
3	means tests	286.3

Source: House of Commons Library Statistical Section

In 1949 means-tested benefits accounted for one tenth of social security expenditure. By 1992 they accounted for around a third. With means-tested expenditure rising at this rate no-one should be surprised that, on the Government's own calculations—and correcting those I gave in *Making Welfare Work*—a third of the population live in households which draw at least one of the major means-tested benefits—Income Support (IS), Housing Benefit (HB), Council Tax Benefit (CTB), or Family Credit (FC). Since 1979 this proportion has doubled.

These figures suggest that expenditure on means-tested welfare is out of control. But the extraordinary fact is that increasing welfare expenditure in this area has been a deliberate plan by the government as part of its strategy to cut the welfare bill. Why has the opposite of what was intended actually happened?

6. Failure of Means-Test Strategy

Means tests do not operate in a vacuum. It is the way in which the eligibility rules for such benefits interact with human character which creates today's welfare disaster. If eligibility for a benefit is determined primarily on the grounds that income or capital is below a statutory level, then a penalty is imposed on honesty, effort and savings. In short, means tests:

- cripple incentives—as income from work rises, means tests bite and benefit value falls;
- penalise savings—people who save are likely to make themselves ineligible for benefits;
- tax honesty—those who are honest about their earnings and savings make themselves ineligible for benefit.

It is here that the Government stands doubly charged with naïvety. They have ignored the way means tests are eroding the values of work, effort, savings and honesty. How long can a society survive once these values are so determinedly undermined in the way that means tests do? But this naïvety about how human motivation will respond to incentives and disincentives is compounded by the Government's expectation of how the spread of means tests will help control the social security budget. Far from limiting claims, each £1 of means-tested benefit helps generate the next £1 claim of benefit.

The National Insurance scheme has been cut back and increasing numbers pushed on to means-tested assistance. The Government claims that this strategy saves money, i.e. fewer people are able to claim benefit. This would be true providing there were no perverse effects. The evidence suggests otherwise.

The Government's view on the impact of benefits is totally static, i.e. what is the impact now on whether or not people claim benefit? Yet people's lives are dynamic, with their circumstances regularly changing. Most partners of unemployed men, for example, give up work when their partner ceases to claim national insurance unemployment pay. The reason for this is quite simple. Once the unemployed person is forced to draw income support, the other partner's income is taken into account. So one office records a fall in the cost of unemployment benefit as a claimant ceases to be eligible. Simultaneously, but unrecognised by the Government's data processing, the same claimant is opening a new account for income support not merely for himself, but often for his family as well.

While one partner remains working, the unemployed partner is looking for a job that pays more than unemployment pay. Once both partners are unemployed the position is transformed. As the likelihood is that only one partner is going to gain a job—at least in the short term—that partner is looking for a wage packet which meets the benefit payments of at least two people. The job search is then confined to employment offering more than the tax-free benefit level for an entire household.

Once both partners are unemployed it becomes increasingly difficult for either to re-enter the jobs market, even if jobs are available. Means tests operate like a vice locking both partners into long-term unemployment and thereby play a crucial role in the emergence of the two-wage-earner/no-wage-earner syndrome.

Means tests also put a claimant's honesty on the rack. Should someone gain a full-time job they are likely to become ineligible for income support (though they may be eligible for family credit if they have children)? Housing benefit is progressively withdrawn as income rises. So too is council tax benefit. Not surprisingly, therefore, a significant group of claimants fail to declare their earnings from work. A growing army of people now regularly cheat their fellow-citizens by claiming benefit while working.

In this way means tests act as the enemy within the welfare state, undermining honesty, work incentives, savings and effort. They also have a ripple effect on the wider society.

Once dishonesty has entered the system—as it now has on a massive scale—means tests help perpetuate and expand claims. The key assumption about social security take-up is that people cease claiming when their need ceases, i.e. when they are no longer unemployed or sick. Means tests positively encourage claimants not to cease claiming, i.e. they penalise work in that the income from benefit is now above the wages of those jobs which claimants with families can realistically expect to gain. Moreover, means tests encourage people to commit fraud, and, once people are claiming fraudulently, fraudulent claims do not usually come to a natural end until the fraud is exposed. This pattern of fraudulent behaviour applies to individual claimants, to landlords and their agents, some of whom have turned housing benefit into a personal merchant bank, and to groups of individuals who are best characterised as a new cult of serious criminal fraudsters.

In addition, considerable numbers of individuals know that the National Insurance system has no foolproof means of checking bogus claims—either by the person using their own number (if they are very simple), the number of someone else, or the number of a person who does not exist. Large numbers of people who are working are also claiming National Insurance benefits, housing benefit, or income support.

Once this dishonesty becomes endemic, the welfare state becomes destabilised. The welfare bills rise as more claimants become eligible while others continue to claim. The Government cuts eligibility for non-means-tested benefits in order to rein back the welfare bill, and thereby forces more people on to means-tested assistance. So the total welfare bill rises yet again and the Government returns to make further cuts ... and that is where the debate currently stands.

Means tests ensure that claimants' energy is channelled into working the system rather than working themselves off welfare. It is in the way they have an impact on effort, savings and honesty that means tests are the most potent recruiting sergeant there is for the dependency culture.

Herein lies a strange political paradox. Means tests provide the nexus of the dependency culture against which the Government so passionately rails. Yet this dependency culture is of the Government's own creation.

7. Means Tests and the Underclass

The underclass is as difficult to define as it is easy to recognise when confronted with it. The major cause is the collapse of full employment and particularly the radically transformed employment position of those with brawn and little developed intelligence. But welfare continues to play a part in both recruiting and solidifying the underclass.

We live in an age where both personal and societal activities are increasingly judged on relative rather than absolute criteria—if judged at all. Within this changed atmosphere we need to set the operation of welfare in respect of how it encourages, sanctions or condones individual actions.

Means tests are of growing importance in today's welfare state and now command a dominant role in the lives of the very poorest. Means tests sanction inaction, non-saving and lying. These powerful messages, relayed through the system which gives basic income support to the poorest, play a part in cutting the poorest off from mainstream Britain. By undermining the character of the poor, means tests also create a fertile ground for the 'yob culture', which again is one of the underclass's distinguishing marks for many male members, and for some females as well. Crime and drugs, themselves often linked together, need to be added. Indeed the underclass, at its strongest point, is fed by unemployment, the abuse of welfare, crime and drugs.

Reconstructing Welfare

Underlying Assumptions

MAKING Welfare Work argued that any reform of welfare which aims for a successful transformation must be based upon:

- a balanced view of human nature
- greater contributor control
- comprehensive coverage
- key socio-economic changes
- the new social culture
- growing social autonomy and its relation to taxation
- the role of trust
- the decline in state power
- the belief in social progress
- new forms of social cohesion.

1. A Balanced View of Human Nature

No welfare system can function effectively if it is not based on a realistic view of human nature. Self-interest, not altruism, is mankind's main driving force.

The view which exaggerated the place of altruism, and which was widely held by Labour activists during the latter part of the post-war period, was a far cry from the beliefs of the founders of the Labour Movement. The latter had a much more rounded view based upon a clear reading of human character. Mankind was (and is) capable of acts of extraordinary altruism, but altruism is generally secondary to self-interest.

To place self-interest at the centre of the discussion is not an amoral—let alone an immoral—act, as some of the Left seem to suggest by their response to *Making Welfare Work*. Nor has it anything at all to do with embracing Thatcherism. It is simply basing welfare policy on realistic assumptions.

Labour's failure to hold a balanced view of human nature presented a picture to the electorate of a party completely out of touch with reality. A party so short on 'street cred' was simply unelectable. But while the distorted view Mrs Thatcher held of the aggressive, self-assertive side of human nature helped to win elections against a politically infantile Labour Party, the negative impact after 17 years of this total focus on self-interest is all around us to see.

A civilised existence often depends on striking the balance between opposing forces. To stress mankind's self-interest to the exclusion of all other attributes ensures that self-interest tumbles into selfishness; and selfishness can itself all too readily collapse into greed.

Part of the necessary moral order is not to do with decrying or thwarting self-interest, but with attempting to satisfy it in a way which is consistent with the public good. The most deadly charge which can be made against Britain's welfare state is that it increasingly ignores this cardinal principle. Welfare is instead pitted against self-interest in a way in which the public good can only be the loser. Hard work is penalised by the loss of entitlement. Incentives reinforce welfare dependency. Honesty is punished by a loss of income. It is in this sense that means-tested welfare is the enemy within. Its rules actively undermine the whole fabric of our character. In so doing it is a cancer within the public domain helping to erode the wider moral order of society.

How should a rightly structured self-interest influence welfare reconstruction? *Making Welfare Work* argued for a stakeholders' welfare which would be increasingly insurance-based. Benefits would accordingly be much more closely linked to the payment of contributions and, with regard to pensions (far and away the largest area of expenditure), *Making Welfare Work* made the case for individuals owning their own capital.

Altruism has a clear role to play in the proposed reform. The structure would be made comprehensive by taxpayers paying the contributions of those people who were unavoidably out of the job market—through unemployment or because they were undertaking caring roles, for example. But *Making Welfare Work* was explicit in arguing that, for the time being, the age of large, unspecified redistributive acts was ended. Politicians who argue otherwise are a public menace. I do believe, however, that hypothecated redistribution is possible within carefully defined parameters. *Making Welfare Work* attempted to define these limits. The redistribution has to be part of the scheme which the majority of the electorate supports for clear reasons of self-interest. Indeed, as *Making Welfare Work* argued, the altruistic element in the scheme had at least a flavour of self-interest about it, i.e. 'who knows which member of my family is going to lose their job again in the euphemistically named growing flexible labour market?' *Making a success of these welfare reforms, with altruism playing an important but subsidiary role, will open up the possibility of building on this altruistic element in further necessary reforms.*

2. Greater Contributor Control

We live in an age of growing individual ownership, a development which has wide support from the electorate. A stakeholders' welfare state will be seen as part of this trend. It fits easily with the actual changes, which will be described shortly, whereby society is moving towards greater social autonomy.

I do not believe, moreover, that a reconstruction of welfare can take place on any other basis. *Welfare expenditure needs to increase in an age of growing demands for tax cuts. That expenditure will not be forthcoming under the existing rules. Voters will support schemes costing more only if they are their own schemes.* No-one now believes that the current National Insurance scheme is theirs, and that the future benefits they are currently paying for are safe. Taking unemployment benefit alone, while contributors have been asked to pay more, the earnings-related supplement to unemployment benefit has been abolished, the eligibility rules have been severely tightened, and, with the Jobseekers' Allowance, the 12 month duration of benefit halved. A new National Insurance scheme controlled by the contributors must be established for voters to believe that their contributions will be safe and that the eligibility rules will not be changed against their interest.

Similarly, increased savings for pensions will be forthcoming only if these savings are individually owned. When old-age pensions, as they were called, were first introduced in 1908, payments were made only to the poorest pensioners aged 70 or over. That was at a time when the average male life expectancy was 48 years! Even after the latest government reforms on raising the retirement age for women qualifying for a retirement pension, the age of qualification will be 65, i.e. five years lower than it was in 1908. Yet this is not a time when only a minority of people reach retirement, and then live at best for a couple of years, as was the case in 1908. Today, practically everybody reaches retirement and lives on for one or two decades or more.

The bill to meet pensions can only be met by transferring a greater proportion of today's income to meet that cost. I do not believe that people will accept the transfer of income that is necessary unless the rules of the game are fundamentally changed. Hence the stakeholder principle, whereby each individual gains ownership over any new assets which are built up in the new scheme.

So, if the welfare debate is considered in traditional terms, and takes into account only levels of government expenditure, the total bill will indeed fall, and with it direct tax rates. But the aim of *Making Welfare Work* was to meet the welfare challenge in the early decades of the new millennium, and that can only be achieved if the amount of income spent on or saved for welfare increases. *But the key to acceptance of this great change is that the speed at which the reform is brought in will be an issue on which individuals themselves will have a say, the welfare institutions will be owned by the participants and the newly accumulated capital will be owned by them.*

3. The Role of Comprehensiveness
The third principle underlying welfare reconstruction is that the new scheme must aim for comprehensiveness and that this objective must take priority over the level or value at which benefits are set. The significance

of this reversal of priorities needs to be stressed. It amounts to no less than a sidestepping of a century-old tradition of British social reform which was touched upon in Section II (*A Pro-poor Campaign*).

In *Making Welfare Work* the term 'comprehensive' was meant to convey how the new welfare state should be inclusive, i.e. including all of the relevant groups and persons. This comprehensiveness was to take clear precedence over the level of benefit. *Making Welfare Work* rejected the idea of defining a poverty line and paying National Insurance benefits above this level which has been the traditional approach of the centre-left. I say 'approach' for it was never realised in government.

Making Welfare Work's objective of ensuring that people are lifted free of means tests also entails, in its initial stages, that the poor who are drawing means-tested assistance gain least from this strategy. For the traditionalist this approach is heresy; instead of delivering most help it delivers least to the poor who are already claiming. *Making Welfare Work* made plain that any successful disengagement from means tests must inevitably result in this outcome; those drawing means-tested assistance will see no immediate increase in their standard of living, while others receive additional help as the new benefit structure begins to take effect. Here is another crunch point where it is vital that the reformer's nerve does not crack. This strategy offers the only realistic possibility of disengaging from means-tested welfare.

This emphasis on comprehensiveness breaks with the British tradition of social reform in a second important respect. The reconstruction of welfare along the lines of *Making Welfare Work* is *not* a readvocation of an exclusive state approach, i.e. providing National Insurance benefits valued at more than an arbitrarily defined poverty line. *The aim is to combine benefit provision with individual and household effort to ensure that living standards are adequate.* This change in direction begins to realign British social policy on a more clearly European line where this general underpinning of living standards is widely supported.

4. Taking Account of Key Socio-economic Changes

The post-war welfare state was designed for a world where a full-time, fully employed male labour force brought home reasonable wage packets, where the traditional family model went unquestioned, where more women worked in the home rather than going out to work, where the overwhelming proportion of young people moved straight from school into work, where once a satisfactory job had been found it would last until retirement some 45 years later, and where retirement was itself of very limited duration.

The world has changed in a number of fundamental ways since the early post-war years, although these changes should not be exaggerated. A clear and accurate view of what has been happening in the labour market, within families and within the country's socio-economic culture, needs to be reflected in welfare state changes.

Revolution in the Jobs Market

There have been three changes in the composition of those in employment which have been billed as near-revolutionary transformations. First, for every woman turning up to work in 1948 there were two male colleagues. Less than 50 years later there were already more women than men working in some industries. Shortly there will be more women working overall.

A second near-revolutionary employment change has been the number of hours worked, and again a significant change occurred in the 1980s. Those in full-time work have maintained the length of their working week, yet the number of full-time jobs has dropped by almost three million. During the same period the number of part-time jobs has expanded by almost a third—or by just under two million.

The third change has been an increase in the number of jobs which make up what has been called the flexible job market, for it is in this part of the labour market that new or re-entrants have to seek employment. Three findings from the work of Paul Gregg and Jonathan Wadsworth are central to the debate.[4]

Whilst in 1992-3 66 per cent of all work consisted of full-time permanent jobs, less than one third of new job placements were of this kind.

The marginal nature of these job openings is reflected in their pay. While the pay of those moving between jobs is clustered midway between half-median and median weekly earnings, the pay of those entering or re-entering the labour market is skewed towards the bottom end of the pay hierarchy. For that group entering the job market the pay of 45 per cent was at a quarter of median aggregate earnings or less, i.e. less than £56 a week, while 55 per cent was below half-median earnings.

New entries into work generally gain less secure posts.

Over 50 per cent of employment inflows are into part-time or temporary employment. Such is the destination too of 65 per cent of those from non-employment. More significantly, only 14 per cent of those leaving full-time temporary work for permanent work are observed in similar full-time positions three months later.

The current system of welfare interacts with the labour market in a destructive manner.

Here we turn to the likely income from work for those on means-tested assistance. Remember the Gregg and Wadsworth finding: 55 per cent of entry jobs paid below half median earnings. The DSS estimates that, in 1991, a couple with children on 75 per cent of median earnings could be gaining only 20 per cent more than their benefit income. Yet only 20 per cent of entry jobs paid 75 per cent of median wages.

With entry wages at this level it is not surprising that Paul Gregg and Jonathan Wadsworth found that a significant change in the likelihood of gaining a job depended upon whether one's partner was in work. In 1979 there was 'a positive differential' in favour of unemployed workers finding work where their partners were also not in work. When this analysis was carried out again in 1985 (and in 1990 and 1993) the non-exit rate was reversed.

In 1979, even if both partners were unemployed, jobs were taken by one of the partners which gained pay levels thought to be suitable in comparison to benefit levels. Now the pay of entry jobs is such that the income from work for that one partner gaining work is below—and often well below—the income of the *household* from benefit. Hence the drive towards the two-or-more-wage-households/no-wage-households. This is a crucial finding which we must take into account when reconstructing welfare.

The Growth in the Number of Single Parents

In 1971, when the only consistent series of data on single parents was initiated, there were 570,000 single parents responsible for one million children. Provisional estimates for 1992 indicate that the total has soared to 1.4 million single parents—a near trebling in the space of a little over twenty years—who are responsible for 2.3 million children.

The reason for this recent growth in the number of children in one-parent families is due largely to the significant increase in the number of never-married mothers. This is now the fastest-growing group of one-parent families—rising from 90,000 in 1971 to 490,000 in 1992, an increase at a rate of eight per cent a year. Overwhelmingly these mothers are young and therefore could become part of a growing group of single parents who are likely to have several children by different partners.

The growth of single-parent families should concern us for a number of reasons.

- Children of single parents are much more likely to be condemned to low income. Children of single parents account for less than one in five of all children. But these children account for very nearly two out of three—1.8 million of the three million—children living on income support.

- More and more single parents are having to resort to means-tested income support. 43 per cent of single parents drew supplementary benefit in 1971. Today that proportion has risen to over 75 per cent.

- Single parenthood is the major cause of family poverty. Single parenthood now far outstrips unemployment as a cause of child poverty. One million single parents claim income support compared to just under 300,000 unemployed parents—less than 30 per cent of the numbers of single-parent families on benefit.

- We do not know the long-term effects for the 2.3 million children currently living without two parents.

How the income support system can be transformed from one which reinforces a single mother's separation from the labour market, into one which becomes a pro-active agency providing a liferaft back into work, constitutes one of the major proposals for reform in *Making Welfare Work* and is detailed later.

New Social Culture

While these are the main changes to the social and economic structure of Britain as they affect people, there is simultaneously a similar ferment in respect of ideas that individuals hold about themselves and the world around them, and these too bear directly on the direction which the reconstruction of welfare has to take if it is to meet with widespread public support.

In her DEMOS report *No Turning Back: generations and the gender-quake,*[5] Helen Wilkinson draws on survey work conducted by Synergy. Politics, including the politics of welfare, will be transformed in a society where the core values of authority, puritanism, security, well-being and connectedness are being replaced by risk, optimism, excitement, escapism and internationalism. And that is what this survey, conducted over a twenty-year period, shows. 18-to-34 year-olds are likely to carry these values into middle age. New generations appear to be even more committed to these values and the lifestyles they embody.

How might these new values be categorised? Individualism, even positive individualism, simply has too much of a backward glance to it. Such a phrase also ignores the new wider networks based on friendship and love which are taking an increasingly central place in people's lives.

An emphasis on individualism also fails to convey both the richness and the geographical spread of many of the contacts which are now important to voters. A small survey in the London Borough of Wandsworth, for example, revealed that, within the first seven months of 1994, 34 per cent of the sample had been abroad, 60 per cent kept in regular touch by telephone with personal friends or family abroad, and that, of this sample, 31 per cent had lived abroad for part of their lives.[6]

Welfare's reconstruction therefore needs to reflect this trend which I can best describe as social autonomy: social because life is very much seen in terms of one's relationships with others—in marriage, partnership and friendship—and autonomous because individuals increasingly want to decide matters themselves. This growing social autonomy is having an impact on—traditionalists would say fracturing—people's attitude to the level of taxation. Both social attitudes and the developments in the economy are giving rise to greater choice.

5. Social Autonomy and Taxation

These two forces are coming together over the question of funding government activities. Economic changes have brought about a shift not only in the type of job, but in the manner in which people are paid. This itself allows more and more individuals a say in how and where they pay taxes, if at all. Two clear forces are at work which limit the scope of government to levy and collect taxes.

An ever-growing army of individuals is able to determine their tax rates over and above the simple choice of deciding what their income will be in any tax year. The very highest earners now have the opportunity to move much of their income out of reach of the taxing authorities, either by creating tax frameworks which minimise their tax liability in their country of origin, or by choosing the most favourable tax regime elsewhere. This reaction by those who corner an increasing share of income is matched by those lower down the income hierarchy. While it is impossible to gauge accurately, the black economy is not merely alive but flourishing.

We are still living through the era when taxes are paid more or less quiescently, because the gains in education, health, and welfare far outweigh what could be purchased individually. The demand is not for root-and-branch dismantling of public services. It is more subtle than that. There is, however, a two-fold response to the continual rise in living standards, and a growing choice which both it and technological advances offer.

There is a growing demand for a say in the provision of public services which would have struck politicians as late as the 1970s as a mark of near-insolence in voters. The age of the *castrati* electorate is fast coming to an end. Here the Tories have caught the direction of the public mood. Indeed, all good left-wingers who support public services ought to be 100 per cent behind rather than mocking the Prime Minister in his drive for public-sector consumer charters. Without this move the force of the second change—the collapse of tax quiescence—will be even quicker and stronger.

As living standards continue to rise voters will want to spend for themselves the gains of increased earnings. This is one of the great forces for change which has all the appearances of growing in importance as time advances.

This drive towards greater individual consumer sovereignty is everywhere to be seen. Michael Young, the person most perceptive of new social trends, has written wittily of how what I have called social individualism functions in strong traditional families.[7]

He reports parents becoming reduced to the role of chauffeurs, motoring their children to individually chosen leisure pursuits, the children sitting alone in the back of a car listening privately to their own portable CDs or Walkmans, rushing up to their own rooms on returning home to continue playing with their computer games, appearing only at intervals to put food into the microwave, to eat alone before returning to the latest phase of their computer game or conversing silently with faceless names on the Internet. It is not only the pressure on building costs which has led to something like a third of all newly built homes having no place where a family could sit down together and eat a meal; there is simply less demand for such an outmoded use of space. This social individualism is also having an impact on how we regard our duties across the generations.

6. Role of Trust

An unspoken assumption about today's welfare state is that of trust. In a pay-as-you-go scheme, where today's contributors do not build up capital sums, but merely pay today's benefit bills, trust that future generations will do the decent thing and continue to pay, so that today's contributors can later draw benefits, is pivotal. Here then is a further great force making for change in financing welfare.

Changing attitudes to trust, and particularly to how it operates through generations, set another framework within which welfare reconstruction has to be set. Far from taking this trust as given—as many left-wing reformers do—I believe we need to consider urgently how it can be supported and nurtured, while accepting that the growing push for greater social autonomy will lead to a re-evaluation of the role of trust in welfare.

The single biggest element of trust in today's welfare state is given in the operation of the state's two retirement pension schemes. Today's contributors pay today's pensions in the expectation that their pensions will in turn be paid largely by an as yet unborn workforce.

Any serious politician would be cautious about placing too much financial pressure on this trust. It could simply fracture. This reason alone should lead Labour to reject ideas currently being put forward about rebuilding SERPS. To go down this route would mean that Labour is making promises to today's taxpayers which it will have no power to deliver from generations of taxpayers not yet born.

A SERPS approach has to be rejected for another reason. It typifies old Labour. Taxpayers are already showing signs of embracing additional pension costs. Very substantial numbers of workers are now covered by second pensions. The argument in *Making Welfare Work* was to make this trend universal by compulsion. What trust there is must be harnessed to help finance a new social security benefit for long-term care.

The demise of a world where trust was so taken for granted that it was never mentioned in public debate does not, unfortunately, complete the list of forces making for a fundamental rethink of Britain's politics. The role of the state is also being questioned.

7. Decline of State Power

Most of today's politicians grew up during those extraordinary years of the twentieth century—the decades of full employment following World War Two. Partly because there was full employment, but for other reasons too, there was a period of optimism about the power of the state. The nation state could, or at least could appear to run the economy, and the state's writ ran throughout our lives; from birth, clinic, school, right up until we were safely delivered into the labour market where there was an abundance of jobs. It looked after us if for any extraordinary reason we were without a job. It also cared for us in old age.

The state no longer has the power to behave in a similarly omnipotent way today, particularly not in the most important of areas—that of jobs. In part this is because its legal writ no longer coincides so obviously with the structure of economic power and decision making—the internationali-sation of companies and communications is increasingly reducing the effectiveness of nation-states. Financial deregulation, which has been taken much further here than in most other countries, allows companies to operate across traditional geographical boundaries.

National governments will increasingly be made prisoners of these wider economic forces. Governments not only appear to be but indeed are helpless in areas of vital concern to their citizenry. Failure to perform effectively further undermines confidence in the state's power. The mechanics of decline are thereby definitely in motion. As governments look less and less powerful and effective, citizens will look elsewhere for services which previously were the province of nation-states. This change should not be over-emphasised. National governments have not been immobilised. But the direction of change is unmistakable. And welfare's reconstruction has to take note of this fundamental shift in the state's power and its ability to deliver.

Coinciding with this gating of the national government's writ is perhaps an even more important revolution which has already been touched upon. Increasing numbers of voters no longer see the state as central in achieving the good life. Indeed, self-achievement is part and parcel of the good life. Consequently a growing proportion of voters now has a changed perception of what legitimately a state not only can, but also should, be expected to achieve. Rather than being the leading player, the state is increasingly cast in the role of an active umpire, setting rules and ensuring that fair play operates. This change alone could have major repercussions on any reform of welfare. But as we have seen it is only one of several forces determining the welfare agenda.

8. Belief in Social Progress

By the end of the Victorian Age there was a widespread belief that, to use Sidney Webb's phrase about socialism, there was something 'inevitable' about social progress. The shock of finding that almost half of inner city dwellers volunteering for the Boer War were unfit for service merely renewed efforts at establishing a national minimum and thereby ensuring progress. Those balmy Edwardian days seemed to promise a continual summer with extension of the Empire overseas and progress at home. Four years fighting in the mud of Flanders fields gave the first serious jolt to the idea that progress was inexorable and that it developed in an unremittingly linear fashion. The response, however, to the catastrophic events on the Western Front was for a renewal of effort. That surely was what was required, given the extent of the sacrifice in the trenches. The idea that progress was not only possible, but was a duty to be pursued, underpinned the moral worth of the Attlee Government. And despite the fact that the electorate naturally, and only too eagerly, moved away from the austerity of the 1940s, the move was towards a society which was offering to spread consumer choice and rising living standards to the majority. Progress was again quickly seen as inevitable and that its effect was to fall like God's gentle rain, uniformly over the entire population.

The Thatcher Government marks a break with this long tradition. Radical change there certainly was. But at the end of that near-permanent revolution the country is left with a marked cynicism about who has benefited from such change. The Thatcher years were marked by sweeping changes, but the benefits in terms of living standards have been concentrated at the very uppermost reaches of the income pile. Progress is no longer seen to be a general movement embracing the whole population.

This has had an ironic political effect; while increasing numbers of people want to dissociate themselves from the Thatcher revolution, there is no great support yet for an alternative. There is widespread agreement about the need for change, but the change is presently more focused on personnel than policy.

Making Welfare Work sought to offer a raft of policies to reform welfare which might help direct this mood for change in a more positive direction. While one of the unspoken assumptions of the book was a reassertion in the belief in social progress, it was a carefully qualified one. It sought to learn the lessons that leading Edwardian reformers tried impress upon politics. Both left and right sought the mechanism which explained the startling social progress that was widely commented upon during the last years of the nineteenth century. The reformers designated the urge for self-improvement as the mainspring of advance and were anxious to ensure that any reforms supported rather than undermined this enabling force in mankind. *Making Welfare Work* debated how this lesson had been lost in the rush for welfare reforms and how best it might regain its pivotal position. It was for this reason that *Making Welfare Work* stressed the importance of welfare reforms being based upon an accurate and adequate understanding of human nature (commented upon earlier in this section).

Making a New Welfare Settlement

A Tripartite Programme

IT WAS against this background of forces which have overwhelmed the post-war status quo that *Making Welfare Work* proposed a tripartite strategy to establish a new welfare settlement.

- Converting income support from a passive to a pro-active agency building, with claimants, pathways to higher skills and re-entrance into the labour market.
- Universalising individually owned pension entitlements which will run alongside the state retirement pension.
- Establishing a new insurance corporation owned and run by the members which will oversee the introduction of new national insurance benefits, starting with unemployment benefit and a new care pension. The corporation's other main function will be to protect these entitlements from government interference.

1. A Pro-active Income Support Agency

The first part of this plan aimed at tackling directly the culture of dependency built up by this Government. In the early days of its drive to herd more and more people on to means-tested assistance, the Government proclaimed every new recruit as an outward visible sign, if not of its compassion, then of its concern for the poor. The atmosphere has markedly changed. Any sense of benevolence has given way to a spiteful stance which blames the victim for the Government's success in railroading people on to means-tested dependency.

If we are to deal with the immediate financial crisis and welfare's dependency culture we must recognise that means-tested income support is the central issue. Indeed the financial crisis and the spread of the dependency culture are, as I have already argued, intimately linked. A government wishing to roll back this culture, and a Labour Chancellor anxious to prevent the welfare budget from imploding, has to consider the means-tested income support welfare budget if the current position is not just to be tinkered with, but radically altered. Moreover, if welfare's bill is to be controlled, and if a higher proportion of its monies are to be spent encouraging values which the wider electorate supports, an attack on the dependency culture about which the Government so hotly rails, while simultaneously spreading that very culture over greater numbers of people, is essential. How can these objectives be achieved?

Rejecting Traditional Anti-poverty Programmes

Making Welfare Work argued for a simple but revolutionary approach. Its plea was for a rejection of the whole strategy which has dominated the poverty agenda since the mid 1960s. From the early years of the Wilson Government the approach has been to devise programmes for helping particular groups of the poor, first by designating very poor areas for priority in government funding, then by singling out particular groups of the poor, such as the unemployed or single parents, and, latterly, targeting only sub-groups, i.e. those who are unemployed for over two years.

As the policy objectives have narrowed, so too have the criteria for what makes a successful reform. The debate, instead of concentrating and advancing first principles, has collapsed into a near obsession with fine tuning the regulations governing entitlement, offering a little incentive here, building a disincentive there. A comparison with the First World War is apposite. When war was declared in August 1914, the expectation was for a quick sweep through France, then on to Berlin, with the troops returning home by Christmas. It was not long before this grand strategy became bogged down in the mud of Flanders' fields. Government ministers look increasingly like those First World War generals whose vision collapsed into a mere obsession over gaining or regaining the next trench. Progress was tortuously slow and the expense unjustifiable. So too with this country's anti-poverty strategy. The whole effort is directed to fine tuning without casting a glance at how the various programmes are impacting on human nature and motivation, both of those groups targeted by reform, and, equally importantly, of those who are excluded.

Moreover, all these modern anti-poverty programmes share a further characteristic. They aim at 'doing good' to the poor. They do not seek to liberate the poor. They aim to control the actions of the targeted group and, consequently, only a limited range of options are offered.

This conventional wisdom about how best to help the poor should be opposed, not simply because it patently has not worked, but also, quite simply, because it no longer meets the challenge. The long-term changes in the distribution of income have had the effect of kicking more and more people down to the bottom of society, and for those at the bottom the prospect of destitution is once again a real possibility.

There is worse to come. The form of help offered is now part of the problem, not part of its solution. The numbers on means-tested welfare grow inexorably. Each means-tested claim helps feed the next. Means tests interact in a perverse and pernicious way on human motivation and thereby on character. Any imaginable welfare state will need a means-tested safety net acting in a limited manner for those without income from work, wealth, or insurance entitlement. That was the role sensibly envisaged by the Attlee Government for means tests. But that emphatically is not what we are faced with today.

The crisis we face is urgent. The hour is late. A dramatic initiative is required which aims not to undermine the growing army of the poor still further, but quite simply to change the political culture in which welfare operates. Moreover the strategy must offer hope to the many rather than the few.

Liberating the Poor

The issue immediately arises of what kind of strategy needs to be adopted if this dual crisis—of finance and dependency—is to be countered. Up until now, all attempts at reform have been piecemeal, targeted efforts. The continuation of such an approach must be resisted. I am not, however, making an appeal for a 'big bang' solution with every aspect of policy changing on a single day. After the Child Support Agency fiasco I simply do not have the courage or the foolhardiness to do so. The CSA crisis has understandably undermined the confidence of reformers. Rather it is a plea for a transformation of income support achieved by a step by step approach. Instead of singling out particular groups of claimants, and doing good to them, the reform is devastatingly simple. Its overall objective is quite simply to set the claimants free.

In 1976 I argued for the mass sale of council houses, and stated that this should be Labour's policy, and that this policy should specifically be presented in terms of freeing the millions of tenants from the serfdom imposed upon them by autocratic local authorities. I now make the same plea for income support claimants. It is time similarly to free them from the bondage of the Poor Law dependency which excludes them from the labour market. *Making Welfare Work's* programme aimed at recruiting an army from those who are conscripted into dependency, turning them into individual agents set on dependency's destruction.

Making Welfare Work's proposal was not for a national programme offering help to single parents, or the unemployed. This segmented approach was rejected. In its place *Making Welfare Work* proposed offering the opportunity to *all* claimants to escape means-tested dependency. It was nothing less than a turning of income support from a passive into a pro-active agency.

Even as a passive agency income support does not score very highly. The Comptroller and Auditor General has qualified the accounts each year since the scheme came into existence. The Agency has two tasks: to pay benefit and to check on fraud, neither of which it does with much finesse. The Comptroller's last report puts the error rate at over 16 per cent for the payment of benefit. In addition fraud is detected in one in ten claims.

Worse still is that income support can only be paid if claimants remain idle. There are examples where this rule does not apply—there are the disregarded sums for those with other income. But the latest figures show that most of this disregarded income is claimed by pensioners, and not by those of working age, so these exceptions make little difference to the tenor of the organisation. It fulfils the main objective of the old Poor Law.

Those now requiring help do not have to enter the workhouse, but an equally telling exclusion is insisted upon. Generally speaking these individuals are excluded from the labour market. It is easy to understand why such a policy might be unthinkingly adopted in the early post-war period when overwhelmingly it was pensioners who sought help from the then National Assistance Board. That is no longer the case, and has not been so for almost two decades. Today, for every pensioner on income support, there are almost five other claimants of non-pensionable age.

Making Welfare Work proposed a fundamental re-ordering of income support, its objectives and the delivery of its benefits for those below pensionable age. The idea that income support should be paid while people await a return to the labour market is no longer appropriate—nor is it a desirable objective in an age of widescale fraud. Breaks in employment are, for all too many, no short spell of idleness, but a condemnation to a long-term exclusion from the labour market.

Making Welfare Work proposed that every claimant below pensionable age and who is fit for work would be expected to plan for what they want to do and achieve during the rest of their working lives. Everyone would be concerned with drawing up a career or life plan. All too many of my constituents have never been accorded the dignity of being asked simple questions about their hopes and wishes for the future, let alone how they might go about to achieve such goals. They therefore have no sense of a goal, a general direction or of any official support in achieving anything. Of course, the scheme could not immediately be brought into universal effect. It would have to be phased in. I have suggested in *How To Pay For The Future* how this plan will work, starting with those aged under 26. This is the group which gains a lower rate of benefit. Even so, I believe the take-up rate will be such that local staff, whose skills will have to be extended to make the reform effective, and combined with the expertise of their job centre colleagues, will be overwhelmed with volunteers. Giving claimants this freedom will itself impact positively on the training programmes which are currently in existence. Claimants will drive the worst of these schemes to the wall as they gain power over choosing their own scheme. In fact many of these schemes should go under, as they are merely providing outdoor relief to the sponsors. Such an outcome should be welcomed.

Income support will be used as an educational maintenance allowance for those going on training courses to help them achieve their career objectives. It will, of course, be necessary to limit further this scheme to those aged under 26 and who have been on benefit for two years. Otherwise there is the danger of the 'Filofax' families tipping their offspring on to income support to ensure that all the stages of further education are paid for by income support grants.

It will also be necessary to link in one further reform. Student grants should be converted into universal loans, run by the private sector, with the sums being clawed back through the tax system. The £1.1 billion thereby released will be used to expand nursery education and child care facilities. There will be no additional revenue costs, but parents on benefit will have the chance of fully participating in the income support liberation programme.

This enfranchising measure will simultaneously achieve a number of key objectives. It will signify that:

- the old system of income support is coming to an end;
- a large part of the dead weight cost of welfare's budget will be turned into an investment budget;
- claimants will have both an opportunity and duty to build their own life rafts from dependency;
- claimants are liberated by this reform which at the same time will act as an effective check on fraud.

Allowing claimants to devise their own exits from benefit will transform the lives of millions who are currently relegated to mere onlookers of their own fate. The reform would also have a major impact on the level of fraud against the DSS. The Comptroller and Auditor General's estimate of fraud in one in ten claims which was cited earlier is, I believe, an underestimate. It is against a proper realisation of the extent of fraud that changes in the running of the DSS must be viewed. The Government's decision to phase out routine home visits had a doubly damaging effect on the efficient running of the Department. Officials involved in visiting claimants in their own homes were able to advise claimants, often pensioners, on their full entitlements. Officers returning to base after such visits would also give fraud officers much information about following up suspected fraud which they had gained only because they had undertaken detailed visits to particular localities.

It is here that the proposal to change Income Support from a passive to a pro-active agency is important. The reform offers real opportunities to claimants planning the next stages of their lives. It will simultaneously act as a massive check on fraud as claimants will be working as officers of the department planning the use of their time, the courses they wish to attend and the jobs for which they applying.

Since this proposal for a pro-active agency was made in *Making Welfare Work* the Social Security Select Committee made a visit to New Zealand to study their pension arrangements. What the Committee found was a less ambitious programme to that proposed in *Making Welfare Work* but one already in operation and working well. Three consequences were very apparent:

- Large numbers of claimants had freed themselves from benefit and moved into work;
- Over two hundred suggestions from staff for further reforms of the social security system have been put into operation;

- Large numbers of claimants when invited for an interview to plan their careers admitted they needed no such plan as they were already in work. This group then left the welfare roll under amnesty arrangements.

The same results I believe would result in Britain if the *Making Welfare Work* proposals for an active agency were implemented. Amnesties should be offered to all those coming forward to close a fraudulent social security account. We would find here that, as in New Zealand, the actual social security budget began to fall, not as a slowdown in the rate of increase which is all politicians have so far offered, but by an actual decrease in the budget in monetary terms. That will be achieved simultaneously with offering claimants the opportunity to plan their own lives. If these plans became effective further falls in the welfare budget would then naturally result.

2. Universalising Dual Pension Provision

The two other major reforms outlined in *Making Welfare Work* attempted similarly to reflect the changed economic and social circumstances of Britain. DIY should not be gated to the home. This approach is one which is fundamentally revolutionising our social, economic and political arrangements. The nature of the good life is changing from one which was exclusively concerned about gaining a certain standard of living to one where the mechanism of achievement became part of the good life itself. The possibilities that this approach holds for most of us, as well as the danger inherent within it for the poor, is illustrated in the pension field where *Making Welfare Work* advocated the compulsory universalisation of second pension provision to run alongside the state retirement pension. The wish for greater choice and control are the forces which have undermined the Attlee welfare settlement. Here the head of steam for change is too strong to oppose—even if one were reactionary enough to wish to do so. But change holds out a real danger for the poor.

As greater numbers withdraw to do their own thing a new pressure will grow on public services. The balance of power will move against those who continue to use the public sector, who will increasingly be the poorest, the least articulate, and those who have gained least from their schooling. As more of the affluent leave the public domain, the pressure will mount for the curtailment of provision until a point is reached when public services disintegrate into a poor law service—so compelling even more to quit its domain.

Direction of Change

This movement is seen most clearly in the pensions field. Here the two movements about which I have spoken have been operating almost unobserved for some considerable time. There is first the disengagement from state welfare as the principal form of income maintenance. The steady movement into occupational pensions has come to an end. But not before the provision of what was so superiorly relegated into the category of occupational welfare has helped transform the retirement prospects of almost half the workforce.

As the occupational pension tide has faltered, its momentum has been garnered by the personal pension market. Despite all the adverse publicity about this form of pension savings, membership has soared. This is a simple but telling fact. It would appear that most buyers of personal pensions know they are being charged excessively for the sale and maintenance of their investment by the company purporting to have sold them a personally crafted pension. Yet the sales continue to tumble in, and they do so despite SIB's failure satisfactorily to bring to an end the mis-selling scandal with the enforcement of adequate rules for compensation. What would be the reaction out there in the market if there existed a cheap and reliable form of pension savings, which also had all the important characteristics possessed by personal pensions, namely, individual ownership of the capital being accumulated? This rhetorical question has simply to be posed. I will return to this issue in a moment.

One measure of the enthusiasm for the ownership of one's own pensions, as opposed to membership of a state's scheme, comes from the stampede out of SERPS. And, despite all the knowledgeable guesses by the grey beards to the contrary, this headlong rush was led overwhelmingly by and composed of younger people. And, of course, personal ownership fits easily with the changes in a labour market where most individuals will have many jobs during their working lives.

This movement out of SERPS was not simply because of the chance to own one's pension capital. That was clearly an element. It was also partly a reaction to a scheme where the writing had been etched on to the wall on more than one occasion. This Government has almost halved SERPS' benefit entitlement, only to half it again. Anyone persuaded that SERPS has a future ought to be made a ward of court. There can be few more certain worse buys at the current time than this scheme.

This disengagement has left SERPS mortally wounded. The scheme acts as a beacon, signalling the dangers awaiting state provision in an age where resistance to tax increases prevents radical improvement in benefit levels. The tide of membership recedes leaving behind many of the most poor and vulnerable. It is easy to decry such developments. It is much more important to consider what can be done.

One set of proposals—to rebuild SERPS—is, as I have argued earlier, a non-starter. These proposals are simply out of time. There does not exist the widespread trust for such a scheme. And trust is only the first of a whole series of necessary ingredients for its success. The number of people who believe that taxpayers not yet born will pay the tax necessary to fund pensions for today's workers in a pay-as-you-go scheme is on the decline. Rebuilding is not a sensible political option.

The Crucial Issue: Including the Poor

What should be done? Immediately we face what is for me the crucial issue on welfare reform. The world is becoming littered with countries reforming welfare, accepting a disengagement from monopoly state provision, encouraging different forms of private provision, and casually allowing the bottom 20 per cent or so to sink into a segregated means-tested poor law type provision. Merely to follow in the wake of these developments would be to surrender Labour's heritage. If the party has stood for anything it has been as a great force for an inclusive society. Here the equality of respect due to each of us is enshrined in our citizenship. And this citizenship is partly defined on the basis of welfare provision, to which each of us earns our entitlement, and will become ever more so if the stakeholder concept is realised in the reform of welfare.

How that provision is provided—whether it comes from the state, private or mutual aid sources—is, I believe, a secondary issue to this fundamental point. To invert the traditional catechismal definition of a sacrament, and refashion it into a political aspiration, the inward meaning of equality is given an outward expression in welfare's incorporation. That incorporation can only come from combining a system of compulsory membership with personal ownership of the welfare capital which results. And this objective can only be made effective by a transfer of money to the poorest outside the labour market, and to those who are low paid, so that their contributions are met and inclusiveness thereby gained. I argue however that this redistribution—a word which radicals should not be afraid to use—needs to be above board, to be clearly of a targeted form, to be made and agreed by taxpayers as a whole, financed by the Exchequer, and on no account paid for by means of a surreptitious filching of funds from individual scheme-holders' accounts.

This takes us now to the important but secondary consideration of how this universal benefit will be supplied. Here I depart from the traditional left thinking in welcoming a multiplicity of suppliers.

New Savings Vehicles

The demand will come from two sources. Those brought into the scheme of funded pensions for the first time will be one source of demand. But there will be at work a larger demand from those already in a personal pension scheme, who realised from the start what a poor buy it was, that it was Hobson's choice, that it was the best available under the restricted circumstances of the time, but who will seize the opportunity to transfer their savings to a more economical vehicle. The ground rules for transferring will have to be considered very carefully by parliament. The aim will be to strengthen the hand of the individual against unwarranted and penal costs imposed by pension companies against those wishing to transfer. The private sector will understandably scream blue—or will it be red—murder on this point. But this is not a new issue. Under occupational pension schemes early leavers were wickedly penalised, and change was forced on the schemes by parliament. So too with private pension provision. Here will be a test for a Blair government in showing that it is not only capable of standing up to vested interests on its own side, but to vested interests wherever they reside. The commitment of the government should be to protect the individual against the corporate vested interest whenever there is a conflict.

One of the criticisms made about *Making Welfare Work's* proposal for universal second pension provision (to run alongside the existing national insurance retirement pension) has centred on the recommendation that these contributions should be compulsory. These critics fail to appreciate that there is already compulsory contribution required for second pension coverage from every worker whose income is above the lower earnings level for national insurance contribution purposes. *Making Welfare Work* was arguing only for a modification of this policy. The suggestion was, first, to bring all workers in, no matter how small their earnings might be in any one year. The second modification now being proposed is to close the pay-as-you-go SERPS scheme and to redirect these SERPS contributions into funded schemes chosen by the contributors themselves. These subsidies to low wage earners for their contributions, and the coverage of pension contributions for those outside the labour market, together with the costs of meeting SERPS entitlements already earned, will be set out in *How To Pay For The Future*.

What should be at the centre of the debate is the form of savings vehicles which will be on offer to attract these new savings and, I believe, much more important in terms of size, the capital already being saved which will become footloose under the reform which allows individuals to disengage from existing high cost personal pension schemes.

Freedom will be the essence. The private sector will be able to compete for these savings. But against them, raising the stakes, will be the mutual aid players. Charges will tumble on two counts. The fierceness of the competition will be one factor. With the advent of compulsion for funded schemes the defence of high charges—large sale forces are necessary to attract the money of unwilling savers—is knocked away. Firms will therefore be forced to attempt to attract trade by the scale of their charges. And the sales emphasis should be at this point rather than by the publishing of bogus figures on likely returns on investment. Indeed the publication of such data should be prohibited. But the mutual aid component will add yet a new cutting edge to these competitive forces.

Rebuilding Social Solidarity

The new era of universal compulsory pension contributions to funded schemes offers the chance of rebuilding, extending and creating new mutual aid organisations. This is not the place to consider the details of these savings schemes. Here rather is the opportunity to spell out the attractiveness of the mutual aid principle, and to consider how a future radical government might ensure that the voice of these bodies is kept above the hubbub of the selling campaign which will understandably be orchestrated by private sector companies.

Mutual aid organisations are membership bodies which build up over many decades a collectively owned business. These are commercially orientated organisations, as concerned with providing an effective service to the customer/investor as is any privately owned body or public company. The vital difference is that in mutual aid bodies there is no group of shareholders to whom dividends are paid. Surpluses are ploughed back into the organisation through lower premiums or more generous benefits, or a combination of both approaches.

The attraction of mutual aid organisations to centre-left politics is such that it is a puzzle why it has not registered more strongly in the current situation. One explanation must be that the period of statist solutions was so total that it had a numbing effect on thinking about alternative ways of providing universal services. Whereas the Blair revolution has overthrown this hegemony, it has yet to rediscover Labour's past and begin prizing those key values which set in motion the beginnings of the socialist commonwealth. These were commonwealths which were not simply dreams which disappeared with daybreak. They were and are a reality. Moreover the reality was not one organised by central bureaucracies, but by the members themselves almost invariably in locally or regionally based groups. Here there was no need to talk of community. Here was the community.

And what was the basis of the flowering of these little and, after a time, not so little mutual aid commonwealths? First, their actions were based on beliefs which are far from inappropriate today. The starting point was simple, namely that acting alone an individual might achieve some gains, but nothing compared to what was possible if those very same individuals worked together. So mutual aid began to change lives—through building societies, co-operatives, friendly societies, savings banks, public libraries and mutual life insurance—long before trades unions became a force, and before parliamentary representation was achieved. Members pooled their resources so homes could be bought—sometimes building them; the quality of food and clothes and household goods were raised through the retail and wholesale co-operatives; and the vagaries of economic life were guarded against through friendly society protection.

Mutual aid both prized but also kept in balance self-interest, that most powerful of human motivations, directing it in a way so that the common interest was simultaneously advanced. Indeed much of its attraction to members must have been that self-interest could only be advanced as part of a collective endeavour. There could not have been a better example of the one strengthening the other.

Mutual aid stands in counter position to the crudities of Thatcherism where only self-interest was valued. It similarly contrasts with Old Labour with its unhealthy and unsustainable emphasis on the primacy of altruism in public policy.

Moreover, the mutual aid movement was not divorced from another of the social objectives of a Victorian period. The emphasis on character, its safeguarding and its advance, was not an idiosyncratic concern of the Charity Organisation Society and similar bodies, no matter how the uninformed left try to suggest otherwise today. Here was a belief which was very much part of working-class culture and aspiration. The mutual aid movement cannot be understood without a proper appreciation of the importance given to the idea of self-improvement. Mankind was thought of in terms of a bundle of abilities and motives with potential which could be developed for good or ill. The mutual aid movement held out the prospect of an organisational form through which members were able to advance their independence and gain over the vagaries of life—of the ever present prospect of being engulfed in poverty, pauperism and the poor law, and of safeguarding themselves and their families from the destructive force which excessive drink brought in its wake.

Above all it was the means by which *de facto* citizenship was attained. 'Working-class we are and our behaviour is equal if not superior to any other class'. That was the proud cry of those who peopled these mutual aid organisations. Indeed, once these self governing organisations began to transform working-class life, on what basis could the franchise be refused? The franchise reforms were merely a public recognition of the citizenship which had already been established by friendly society and mutual aid activities and actions.

The responsibility for self-improvement was clearly located. It rested with individuals themselves, although it was sought through co-operative effort. So again our forebears have a crucial lesson for us about the meaning of how successful social advance is gained. The individual was not demeaned as he or she is by so much of today's left wing ideology which puts all the emphasis on structural causes as the reasons for preventing personal advance. But neither was it naïve in believing that the structural forces were without importance. Again a proper sense of balancing both these arguments was, I believe, achieved.

3. New National Insurance Schemes

Making Welfare Work proposed establishing a stakeholder's national insurance scheme to run in the first instance a new system of unemployment insurance, as well as introducing a new care pension. The ownership of this scheme will need to pass from the Government to the contributors. The reason is quite simple. Contribution rates have been increased but benefit entitlement cut under this Government. National insurance sickness benefit has to all intents and purposes been abolished. Unemployment benefit has been reduced, the earnings-rated supplement abolished and the qualifications for benefit made more stringent. Finally a 12 month right to benefit has been slashed in half as part of the Government's Job Seekers' Allowance reform.

The collective savings on the unemployed (of crucial importance, of course, to each individual) pale into insignificance when compared to the loss suffered by pensioners both individually and as a group. The link to review pension levels in line with earnings or prices has been changed to indexing pensions to price increases only. The savings on this move since 1979 now total £75 billion. Yet, amazingly, had the rates of national insurance contributions from 1978/9 remained in force, £26.5 billion less would have been collected.[8] Put another way, benefits have been cut across the board but contributions have been increased. The national insurance fund has been used as a cover to raise funds for the very significant post-1979 tax cuts to the very richest in Britain.

New Unemployment Benefit Insurance

One of the most striking changes in the working of the labour market has already been described. Since 1979 the wages paid to re-entry jobs have collapsed. Almost half of the jobs which go to those re-entering work pay less than a quarter of median earnings: i.e. below £56 per week in 1990.

Now consider the benefit system. Unemployment benefit which was paid for twelve months has, since April, been cut to six. During this time a wage-earner picks up £48.25 a week without questions being asked about a partner's earnings. The search is therefore for a job which pays above, and hopefully well above, the benefit level. Now consider what happens when there is no insurance benefit. A means-tested income is only offered after taking into account the partner's earnings. The benefit income of £150 plus from income support and housing benefit is more than the income most partners would gain from work. It is deducted pound for pound from any of those earnings except for a miserly disregarded amount. The outcome is obvious. The partner gives up work too. It pays her to do so. She is reacting as a rational economic person. But once out of work what chance is there of either partner finding a job paying more than benefit? Remember those re-entry jobs—almost half below £56 a week? Here then is the basis of the work/no-work households, and it will be made much worse as the duration of the insurance benefit against unemployment benefit has been cut from twelve to six months with the introduction of the new Job Seeker's Allowance.

How To Pay For The Future lays down the basis for a stakeholder's national insurance scheme where those taking re-entry jobs, which often have a short shelf life, are rewarded for so doing. They will quickly requalify for insurance benefit. Risk-taking is therefore rewarded. Families are kept off means tests. Long-term dependency is countered rather than encouraged by the benefit system. Work is more evenly spread throughout the community. Household income thereby becomes more equitable and a start is made simultaneously in closing what has been the widening income gap which has so disfigured Britain, particularly since 1979. The National Insurance Stakeholder reform sets the scene for curtailing the spread and then for the reduction in means-tested welfare.

Care Pension Insurance

Practically everybody will draw a pension. Only a small minority of us will require paid care at the end of our lives. This fundamental difference in our needs should be reflected in the welfare state. While everybody needs to save for their retirement, it is absurd to insist that savings also take place to cover the cost of long-term care which five out of six individuals on current estimates will not need. Here, in fact, is an emerging need which can most effectively and cheaply be delivered by way of a new national benefit, although one which is again kept outside the declining state welfare system. A national insurance benefit has the maximum advantage of re-inforcing the value of inheritance.

The values being promoted by welfare reform need to be flushed out and stated clearly. On the question of inheritance *Making Welfare Work* was unequivocal. The rich, except for the very foolish or the twisted, have always been able to pass on capital from generation to generation. Now, with rising national income, and a genuine property owning democracy, inheritance, albeit much on a more modest scale, is within the grasp of a clear majority of the population. *Making Welfare Work* believed that the opportunity for a very significant group of the population to build up a capital base should not be lost through penal welfare confiscatory rules. *Making Welfare Work* saw inheritance as one of those unappreciated webs so binding families and friends together that individuals are knitted into society, both horizontally, i.e. to people living now, and vertically, gaining from the past and handing on capital into the future.

Moreover, *Making Welfare Work* saw as a highly undesirable outcome the creation of a class of grandparents who misreport their assets in order that they evade welfare's confiscatory rules. *Making Welfare Work's* welfare model for the millennium is one where income is gained from work, capital and welfare—in that order.

Making Welfare Work proposed establishing a new care pension. The scheme would be based on compulsory insurance and run by the new national insurance corporation. The risks of needing care, and the consequent costs, would thereby be spread over the entire population. There will be no possibility of individuals being rejected for membership, as there is in private insurance schemes, either overtly, or via penal premium rates. *How To Pay For the Future* includes the Government Actuary's costings of this reform.

In proposing a reconstruction of welfare in *Making Welfare Work* unemployment insurance and a new care pension were chosen to initiate the insurance scheme. Here the maximum impact could be made in respect of unemployment insurance by preventing an entire household from being without work. The new unemployment insurance would link previous efforts at work to benefit. It would also prevent other members of the household from feeling it necessary to work and lie about their earnings as the incentives in a means-tested scheme presently teach claimants.

Similarly the introduction of a care pension would change people's expectations. Under the present system of a means-tested community care programme, all of the incentives deter claimants from saving, or from being honest about the value of their assets.

Making Welfare Work saw the building up of capital ownership amongst as wide a group of the population as possible as a sign of a successfully strong and vibrant society. Far from viewing life as something entirely self-sufficient, where each generation is expected to produce and consume its entire produce, *Making Welfare Work* saw the strong links between familial generations as fundamental to any group which wishes and is able to consider itself a society. Means tests, applying as they do against income and capital, strike at the very heart of this concept of the good society.

****

The arguments in this discussion draw heavily on the material presented in *Making Welfare Work* where there is a full list of references. The references cited are those which either give specific quotations, or have not been cited in the earlier publication. A fuller argument for the next stage of *Making Welfare Work's* argument will appear in *How To Pay For The Future*. This will include data from the Government Actuary on the costings of the proposal. See order form adjacent to back cover.

44

Notes

1 "Things fall apart; the centre cannot hold; Mere anarchy is loosed upon the world", Yeats, W.B., 'The Second Coming', *Yeats's Poems*, London: Papermac, 1989.

2 Bowley, A.L., *The Nature and Purpose of the Measurement of Social Phenomena*, London: P.S. King, 1923.

3 Bosanquet, N., *Public Spending into the Millennium*, London: Social Market Foundation, 1995.

4 Gregg, P. and Wadsworth, J., 'A Short History of Labour Turnover, Job Tenure, and Job Security, 1975-93', *Oxford Review of Economic Policy*, Vol. 11, No. 1, Oxford: Spring 1995, pp. 73-90.

5 Wilkinson, H., *No Turning Back: Generations and the Genderquake*, London: DEMOS, 1995.

6 Albrow, M., *Globalization: Myths and Realities*, Roehampton Institute, November 1994.

7 Hansard, HC., 20 March 1996, col. 238.

8 Field, F. and Owen, M., 'Private Pensions for All: squaring the circle', *Fabian Society Discussion Paper*, No. 16, London: 1993; and 'National Pensions Savings Plan: universalising private pension provision', *Fabian Society Briefing*, No. 1, London: 1994.

Commentaries

Welfare and Self-interest

Pete Alcock

The Crisis in Welfare

WELFARE and the future of social protection are very much back on the agenda for social policy reform in Britain. After almost two decades in which welfare reform has been regarded as a secondary issue behind the predominant focus upon the securing, or encouraging, of economic growth, this is to be welcomed. Despite the claims of some on both the right and the left that economic growth and social protection are mutually exclusive matters of political priority, there is a wealth of academic evidence and political experience—most especially from continental Europe—that the pursuit of both can reinforce social stability rather than undermine it. This is a perspective which I share; and it is one which I suspect Frank Field shares too—although, as I shall return to argue shortly, it is not one which comes out clearly enough in his recent prescriptions for the welfare society of the new millennium.

However, welfare is not back on the political agenda because of shared assumptions about its central role in the development or maintenance of social stability—quite the reverse. Welfare is on the agenda because in a number of senses welfare is in crisis; and this crisis is borne in large part out of the contradictory experiences of a welfare state which has been experiencing not economic growth but economic recession and restructuring. In a nutshell, these contradictory experiences can be reduced to three predominant problems with welfare in Britain in the 1990s:

- the *cost* of social protection is rising—despite numerous cuts in provision the overall budget continues to grow;
- the *delivery* of protection is failing—too many people are inadequately protected by current welfare measures;
- the *legitimacy* of welfare is questioned—there is no consensus on the desirability of the welfare state.

Questions are being asked therefore about whether we can continue to provide collective welfare protection through the state, and about whether we should. It is in response to these questions that Frank Field has boldly undertaken to produce a blueprint for welfare in the next millennium. His answers, he believes, are both radical and realistic; and they challenge the old welfare shibboleths of both left and right. My concerns are that, though radical in some respects, they do not go far enough in challenging the welfare crisis of the 1990s; and that, though premised on a hard-headed assessment of the potential for reform, they do not produce proposals that could be delivered within the political straight-jacket which Field sets for himself.

Field's challenge to both the New Right and the Old Left is his assertion that the world has changed since the time when the current welfare state was constructed in the 1940s, although the standard critics and defenders of state welfare do not fully recognise this. Beveridge's vision of comprehensive and collective protection for all through a state mechanism, which all would support because all would benefit, both directly and indirectly, from it, has been very widely discredited.

This is in large part because the Thatcher years of the 1980s saw a sustained political assault upon the both the state and the principles of collectivism, as a result of which the values of altruism, social obligation and social citizenship were replaced by the values of individualism, self-interest and private market purchasing. Field has criticised the consequences of these significant changes before.[1] However, he now claims to recognise that the initial post-war welfare settlement was in itself flawed in its comprehensive appeal, permitting the initial drift towards selectivity which has accelerated so rapidly over the past fifteen years. He also challenges the altruism which was so central to the welfare ideal—'self-interest, not altruism', he claims here (p. 19), 'is mankind's driving force'. Thatcherism may have sealed the fate of the post-war welfare state; but its fate, Field suggests, had already been determined by the false premises in its initial creation.

Thus in the 1990s we do not have social protection, but rather social exclusion and social polarisation. These are now recognised increasingly widely as problems in modern society which fundamentally affect us all—not just those excluded or at the bottom of the unequal distribution of resources. However, the solution to these problems is not seen to lie in the collective state protection which it had once been assumed would prevent them. We cannot, it is claimed, recreate the welfare consensus of the post-war period, therefore we must look to something different if we are to make welfare work in the next fifty years or more. Something different has been propounded by the right—notably the authors of previous publications by the IEA. Something different is now being propounded by Field from, he claims, the centre-left. Both share their diagnosis of the failure of collective welfare by the state, though, as I shall briefly summarise, in responding to this they rather part company. Both, however, have mis-diagnosed the condition, or the crisis, of state welfare, and in their different forms of radicalism are risking discarding the baby along with the bathwater of collectivism. Some of the bathwater should perhaps go—if it has not already gone—but the baby must be kept, and must be permitted to grow once again.

The Right's Agenda

The new right critique of state welfare is now quite well-known. Its most eloquent, and perhaps most extreme, proponent has been the American political scientist Charles Murray.[2] A similar, if more measured, argument has been developed in this country within the IEA by David Green.[3] Central to the new right argument is the belief that state welfare cannot be the *solution* to the crisis in welfare, because it is its *cause*. State welfare interferes with the freedom of people to consume their wealth and income as they think fit within a free market, and it involves unjustified, unpopular and expensive control over our current resources and our future plans. State welfare also creates perverse incentives, encouraging dependency and stifling self-protection and initiative. State welfare therefore takes control over people's lives away from individuals and communities: the new right answer is to return this control by taking away instead state welfare.

In their proposals to remove state welfare writers such as Murray and Green draw support from a developing communitarian agenda, advanced particularly in the US by Etzioni.[4] State welfare can be withdrawn, it is argued, because communities can be expected to provide welfare support for themselves: it is what they did before the advent of state welfare, it is what they would prefer to do after it. Such community-based welfare support is desirable because it lacks the interference with freedom and the perverse incentives of state welfare; and it is feasible because we know that it worked in the past, as in Britain in the nineteenth century.[5]

In this sense, however, the new right agenda for the removal of state welfare is very much a case of 'back to the future'—an attempt to recreate the community support of the past in a post-welfare state future. This is at best an untried strategy, and at least a risky one. Green himself is not prepared to risk the complete withdrawal of state welfare on it, and proposes still the retention of some state protection as a safety net. Murray has always been stronger on critique than on construction, and does not spell out a clear strategy for a return to community support. It is in fact highly unlikely that the community organisations of nineteenth century Britain would re-appear at the end of the twentieth century, and much more likely that Green's safety net would turn out—just like Beveridge's safety net of social assistance within the state social security scheme—to become the predominant form of social protection; but that is a debate for another place and time. Where it is relevant to discussion of Frank Field's proposals for a new approach to welfare in the twenty-first century is in the assumptions which the new right agenda shares with Field about the communitarian agenda and the potential strength of community-based alternatives to state welfare protection. There are some interesting similarities here; but also some important differences.

Field and the Centre-Left

The centre-left with which Frank Field now wishes to associate himself is the *New Labour* Party of Tony Blair—although Field has in the past shown himself to be too individually minded to be a central figure in Blair's increasingly close inner circle of advisors and potential senior cabinet members. New Labour is a party of partnership rather than state domination, in which secure funding rather than redistribution is at the top of the public spending agenda. Field distinguishes this from old Labour's 'unhealthy and unsustainable emphasis on the primacy of altruism' (p. 40) with its reliance upon redistribution through public support.

The distinction which Field is implicitly drawing here is one between the 'optimistic' altruism and welfare statism of Titmuss and the supposedly more realistic vision of social obligation and mutual support identified by Tawney—a distinction also drawn out by Deacon in Chapter Two. It is interesting, and perhaps not coincidental, that Tawney—like Field and Blair—was outspoken about the Christian base of his social vision. Christian Socialism has always been a powerful subculture within British Labourism, and at the end of the century its influence is likely once again to play a prominent part in policy development in Britain—although it is far from clear that this would, or should, lead to a withdrawal from altruism or collective protection through the state.

Field is not just a Christian, however. He is a well-known Labour radical and a dedicated Parliamentarian. He is also one-time Director of the Child Poverty Action Group; and following this still a tireless campaigner for social security reform. Furthermore, he is one of the few MPs who can claim a genuine understanding of the intricacies of social security policy. His analysis of welfare problems and his prescriptions for benefit reform are therefore taken seriously by all shades of political opinion—and rightly so. For in *Making Welfare Work*, as in all his previous recommendations, they are based on a sound and detailed appraisal of what is wrong.

What is wrong with social security policy in Britain in the 1990s, Field correctly argues, is the over-reliance which is now experienced on means-tested benefit support. Means-tested benefits produce in their sharpest form the perverse incentives of benefit dependency, creating various forms of contradictory, yet inevitable, traps for those (now one third of the population) caught within them.

- An *unemployment trap*—the wages to be found in many of the jobs on offer means that these will not replace the income received from means-tested benefits, especially for those with families to support.

- A *savings trap*—the requirement that capital resources are used to reduce benefit entitlement means that those with savings, especially the elderly, will see no additional income from these.

- A *poverty trap*—the use of benefits to supplement low wages means that those in low paid jobs cannot improve their circumstances by moving up the income scale.

As Field points out, these are unavoidable features of means testing—they can only be prevented by moving away from means tests as the basis for determining entitlement to state support. Relegating such benefits to 'safety net' role, as suggested by Green[6] or by Beveridge,[7] will not work unless a comprehensive alternative is developed.

It is in facing up to this dilemma in the condition of social protection in Britain that Field is genuinely taking a radical stand. Challenging the disincentive culture of means testing requires a head-on assault and a clear policy alternative—the time for tinkering has long past, albeit that governments seem continually to seek to return to it.

Field's proposals for welfare reform thus stem from a hard-headed assessment of the current problems of social security provision; and in this sense they are both radical and realistic,

- *radical* in that they require a major shift in the direction of policy development;
- *realistic* in that they seek to develop policies which could be sustained within current political parameters.

As I shall return to discuss, however, both the radicalism and the realism of Field's prescriptions for the reform of social security can be questioned.

Field's proposals for welfare reform are also drawn, however, from his rejection of old Labour altruism and the commitment to redistribution through the state. His belief is that people will no longer support state policies for redistribution unless they are likely to benefit as individuals from them, and that the altruism of collective protection has been—or should be—replaced by an emphasis instead upon mutual self-help and responsibility. What is required, Field claims, is a 'remoralisation of welfare' and the adaptation of collective protection to reflect the driving force of self-interest. Field's proposals therefore stem from questions of moral responsibility (embracement of Tawney's notion of obligation as well as benefit) and political judgement (belief in the political improbability of redistribution) as well as the need for practical reform (replacement of the disincentive culture of means testing). As such they do constitute a holistic vision, but one which rests on questionable assumptions in each part. Thus his prescriptions for a new welfare settlement are based on a plan which will not work within the conditions which Field has set for it.

Moral Responsibility

A major element of Field's view of the need for a remoralisation of welfare stems from his acceptance of the 'driving force' of self-interest in structuring human society. This may not be quite the same thing as the adoption by economists of the idealised notion of the rational and self-maximising person as the basis of all social intercourse, but it does involve a similar, and unsubstantiated, level of abstraction from the complexity of real social relations. Field does not explain why human individuals should be self-interested rather than altruistic, nor why they could not in practice be both—although there is much evidence from history to suggest that this might indeed be the case.

It may be, of course, that Field has been influenced here by the Thatcherite agenda of the 1980s, of which he has elsewhere been so critical. After more than a decade in which the needs and desires of the individual have been openly championed over the collective values of social welfare it is perhaps not surprising that individualism should appear as the driving force of social order—most graphically revealed in Margaret Thatcher's oft quoted claim that 'there is no such thing as society'. However we should all, including Field, be wary of taking the public pronouncements of government as a proxy for the real views and values of people: our electoral system is not that sensitive or that responsive. Individualism may be politically dominant; but that does not mean that it has become a permanent social state. Such dominance could, and should, be challenged.

Field's attachment to individualism is probably the consequence of deeper commitments within his approach to welfare, however, and owes its roots here to his Christian communitarianism as much as to his experience of 1980s British anti-collectivism. Field extends his analysis of the contrast between mutual self-protection (self-interest) and social collectivism (altruism) back to the debates in the early twentieth century between the majority and minority reports of the Poor Law Commission—dominated respectively by the Bosanquets and the Webbs.[8] He contrasts the 'state collectivism' of the Webbs to the 'popular collectivism' propounded by the Bosanquets.[9]

For the Bosanquets, and the Charity Organisation Society (COS) with which they were associated, social protection was best provided by mutual self-help and was intended to include clear moral obligations on behalf of the recipient to seek to contribute and on behalf of the provider to impose a moral regime. Such social protection was not necessarily best provided by the state therefore, but might better be organised through third sector organisations such as the friendly societies. The subsequent development in the later twentieth century of state-based welfare, rooted more closely in the altruistic ideas of the Webbs, in effect saw this model predominate over the mutual self-help of the friendly societies in Britain—and elsewhere. This is a matter of regret to Field, and perhaps also for him a cause of the ultimate crisis within the state welfare model.

Thus it is with the responsibility and mutuality of the friendly society ethos that Field wishes to remoralise welfare at the beginning of the twenty-first century; and it is in this sense that his agenda for reform overlaps to some extent with that of the new right.[10] Both Green and Field see an enhanced role for the third sector here, and an enhanced role for morality in the delivery and receipt of welfare; but this is a dangerous road to go down—especially if it is followed at the expense of continued support for the traditional, and altruistic, role of the state in guaranteeing social protection.

Mutual self-help can be exclusive as well as inclusive. The friendly societies and approved insurers of the nineteenth and early twentieth centuries generally had very clear views of their target populations; and these did not include many who might desperately need protection. In a socially and culturally divided society such as modern Britain welfare based on mutual self-help could reinforce social exclusion based on ethnicity, age, disability, gender and other social divisions. At least in an inclusive state model, driven by a commitment to collective protection through redistribution, it can be argued that those who are excluded—as unfortunately many still are—should be brought within the welfare net. Mutual self-help is not amenable to such moral persuasion.

Thus mutual self-help and the morality of individual responsibility does not guarantee the provision of a vehicle for ensuring social protection for all. For this a commitment to altruism is also needed. Yet Field recognises, and wishes to incorporate in his reforms, such altruistic redistribution—for instance, in his proposal for a Care Pension Insurance which is explicitly modelled on a state-based form of redistribution in which benefit will be based on need, not contribution, and only some will ever get to benefit. This is probably a good way of providing support for those who need care, but it will only be successful if organised through the state and supported for altruistic reasons.

Political Judgement

Despite relying on support for redistribution through the state for his care pension, however, Field is generally of the view that the basis of political support for redistribution through the state no longer exists in Britain at the end of the twentieth century—'the age of large, unspecified redistributive acts [h]as ended' (p. 20). This is because, like New Labour more generally, Field accepts the view that electoral success can only be built upon promises of reductions in personal taxation. The old Labour social democrats and socialists who argued for fiscal policy to reflect visions of social justice and social protection (the 'levellers' as the Borrie Commission on Social Justice called them)[11] are now political pariahs—or to use Field's language, 'a public menace' (p. 20).

That the taxation promises of most governments—not the least John Major's 1990s administration—have owed more to political rhetoric than social and economic planning is something we can perhaps skate over here. Suffice it to say that many people may be more than prepared for a gap between rhetoric and reality here. Nevertheless it is far from clear why Field should accept the inevitability of the low taxation policy agenda, or on what evidence he bases this judgement. Field has been known in the past to use consultations and conversations with his constituents in Birkenhead as evidence of the development of political trends. This may be laudable constituency practice, but it is a rather partial sample to act as a basis for political research.

The cynical judgement may well be that Field's commitment to the low taxation agenda is a blatant case of swimming with the tide of political debate within the Labour Party, especially linking it, as he does, to the 'stakeholder' concept of future social reform. But Field has often in the past demonstrated a stubborn willingness to struggle against even the strongest Labour tides, so I am inclined to give him the benefit of the doubt on this issue. More likely, perhaps, Field's judgement is once again clouded here by the cumulative experience of the Thatcherite political snowball. The message that low taxes equal economic growth equal political popularity has been so consistently repeated by politicians and media pundits that many, including Field himself, have perhaps begun to believe that it must be true.

However, this is far from the case. For a start economic growth and political popularity could hardly be said to be the main characteristics of British government in the 1990s; and as academic research by experts such as Hills has shown it is not low taxation, but rather low *direct* taxation that has been the only consistent fiscal priority of recent governments.[12] In fact, what has happened to Britain over the last fifteen or so years is that the country has become much more unequal across a range of dimensions; and much of this increased inequality has been the direct result of social and economic policies aimed at redistribution of resources. Yet at the same time economic growth has been slow compared to most of our nearest economic competitors.

Therefore governments can redistribute resources, even in recessions, and they can use fiscal measures to achieve this. This is just what the Thatcher governments of the 1980s did. Unfortunately (for many) this redistribution ran from poor to rich, rather than the other way round, and yet political support for this was developed and sustained by government. The political lesson to be learnt from this, however, is not that redistribution in another direction is politically impossible—rather that alternative political support for it needs to be developed.

Certainly there is scope for redistribution towards the poor which could make Britain a much less divided and polarised society in the early twenty-first century. The Government's own figures on income distribution, the Households Below Average Incomes (HBAI) figures,[13] supplemented by the recent Rowntree research on income and wealth,[14] provide clear evidence of a potentially popular agenda here. The most recent HBAI figures show that between 1979 and 1992/3 the numbers of people receiving below 50 per cent of average income rose from five million (nine per cent) to 14.1 million (25 per cent): there are many more people at the bottom. They also show that over the same period the real incomes of those at the bottom (after housing costs) *fell* by 17 per cent, whilst the average income grew by 38 per cent and the incomes of those at the top grew by 62 per cent. The rich have gained a lot from economic growth and the poor have lost out.

Presenting a case for reducing the numbers at the bottom and redistributing resources from those who have gained a lot to those who have lost out over the last fifteen years would not be based on the political judgement of a 'public menace'—although it would be based on the morality of altruism. However, a political judgement which assumes that such arguments are *prima facie* to be ruled out of court is seeking to restrict political debate, as well as to handicap policy reform. Redistribution is not politically impossible, nor politically unpopular—rather it is a political priority. And it is just as well that it is, because in practice the welfare reforms proposed by Field would require significant amounts of redistribution through the state if they were to be implemented—although it is debatable whether they should be the first priority for such redistribution.

Practical Problems

Alongside his arguments for a new moral order in welfare and his critique of the deficiencies of the current predominance of means testing within social security protection, Frank Field outlines some fairly detailed proposals for the practical reform of benefit policy. Field's great strength as a politician and campaigner is that he is not just a moraliser, still less a party hack. He has clear and practical recommendations for reform which draw on his considerable knowledge and experience of social security. I will not repeat these proposals here, but merely summarise a few key points:

- Extend National Insurance (NI) cover by retaining and strengthening the insurance principle but using state resources to credit in some of those currently excluded from protection; and establish NI as an independent non-government organisation.

- Develop a partnership with the private pensions industry to provide a comprehensive private sector pension for all, replacing SERPS, using state resources to pay the contributions of those who cannot afford private coverage themselves.

- Institute a new National Insurance Care Pension to provide for the costs of those needing personal care later in life, financed by contributions from all.

- Restructure the delivery of Income Support (IS) so that it operates as an individual counselling and advisory service for all unemployed people (including lone parents), ensuring that all job vacancies are notified to the state run Job Centres, and cracking down on fraud.

These are radical, though not revolutionary, reforms. With sufficient political will and administrative commitment they may be achievable. However, they contain some worrying problems and contradictions.

The extension of NI is proposed by Field as the main vehicle for the gradual replacement and demise of means testing (nothing new here, however); and yet he proposes to retain relatively strict contribution tests within a revitalised insurance principle to determine entitlement to NI benefits. Indeed the establishment of NI as a separate agency is intended to underline the conception of NI benefits as a protection purchased, and owned, by NI contributors. This involves the creation of yet another massive and powerful QUANGO, and one with control over a large part of public expenditure. It also means a continuation of the exclusive, and exclusionary, nature of NI protection. Contribution tests only have any meaning if some are excluded by them. What is to happen to those so excluded? The answer is that they will remain on Income Support, and this has disturbing connotations of *deja vu*.

However, to avoid too many being excluded, Field proposes to use state resources (taxpayers' money) to credit in some who cannot make their own contributions. This retains the fiction of insurance in principle, only by avoiding it in practice. Is all this subterfuge necessary, or desirable? More importantly it involves significant state expenditure, or redistribution, to provide cover for those so credited—likely to be, of course, the low paid and marginal employees at the bottom of the labour market. Such redistribution is laudable—and desirable—but it is not mutual self-protection, and it will incur significant expenditure (and taxation) commitments. Yet these are the very things which Field claims earlier are morally and politically unacceptable.

Much the same expenditure and taxation commitments are hidden (or not-so-hidden) within Field's other supposedly practical policy reforms. The care pension is self-confessedly based on new contributions and a redistributive model of protection. The new public/private second pension will require significant public resources to purchase pension rights for the low paid, no paid and unemployed. The new individualised Income Support, welfare into work, scheme will have major administrative costs if it is to move from being a depersonalised bureaucracy to becoming an individual source of support for self-development. Field claims that the more efficient identification of benefit fraud will bring about a major saving in benefit costs here, although his predictions are rather non-specific on this—and some might say rather optimistic.

Therefore, despite the protestations to the contrary, Field is proposing welfare reforms which will have significant public expenditure and taxation implications and will use this expenditure to redistribute resources largely to people currently excluded from private insurance and NI protection. Yet at the same time Field is openly critical of the morals and the methods by which such redistribution might be justified and achieved. If self-interest and mutual benefit are at the heart of all human motivation, how can people be convinced to support increased taxation in order to buy insurance protection in the public and private sectors for people who cannot afford to pay for it themselves? And if individual responsibility and self-support are the moral tenets of protection for the unemployed, how can people be persuaded to finance a system of income support which provides individual counselling and life course planning for unemployed people who are outside the insurance scheme?

The answer to these questions is, only surely if they can be convinced that the provision of public support through collective protection is a moral duty and a social good. In other words only if they can be convinced that altruism is a legitimate, and a necessary, basis for the development of welfare protection; and that this will require redistribution from rich to poor—rather than the other way round. This is an old message, at least as old as Titmuss and the Webbs, but it is not an outdated one. Fifteen years of Thatcherism may have driven altruism down the political agenda but they have not killed it off.

A Social and Economic Strategy for Welfare

In addition to its contradictory, and self-defeating, message on redistribution, there are some other problems with Field's proposals for the reform of social security protection through National Insurance, especially in terms of its consequences for the unemployed. For a start it is not clear whether his proposed partial extension of NI protection would mean that those benefiting from the improved insurance cover would be those most likely to perceive this as an improved incentive to seek paid work. For instance, if insurance cover is extended to the unemployed partners of unemployed men this is likely simply to transfer benefit expenditure from the IS to the NI budgets. This would be a useful and important step for gender equality, but it would not redistribute new money to the poor and it would not change the dynamics of the labour market.

More importantly perhaps it is far from clear that a new and more personalised regime of support and encouragement for the unemployed on Income Support would be the most practical way of challenging the problems of long-term unemployment and benefit dependency. Like most social policy, and especially social security policy, analysts Field has approached the problem of unemployment from the point of view of the unemployed—just as he has approached the question of inequality from the point of taxation and benefit income transfers. This is a focus on labour supply not demand, and upon the results of the distribution of resources rather than their cause. If we wish to achieve real, and effective, changes to the problems of unemployment and inequality in modern society we have to take a broader policy perspective, and focus attention at policy intervention earlier in the economic cycle. This is just what many economists—though few politicians—have consistently argued.[15]

To put this in more practical terms, changing incentives and encouragement for the unemployed will not provide them with jobs, still less adequately paid ones. Field himself knows how few jobs are on offer, and how many of these are on terms that will not provide for the obligations of many potential workers. This situation can only be altered by intervention in the labour market, not further exhortation of those outside it. This means strategies for job creation, investment planning, and labour market regulation—including the imposition of minimum wages. Such measures require an economic, as well as a social, strategy for reform—indeed they require that both be developed together. They also imply the tackling of the inequitable distribution of resources at a point before taxation and benefit policies begin to take effect—minimum (and maximum) wages would reduce initial inequalities within the labour market, and improved job prospects would change the balance between those within it and those outside.

Of course these are not matters for social security policy *per se*; and Frank Field might justifiably argue that they are beyond the brief of his plans for welfare reform. But the point is that it is only by extending the frame of reference of policy reform in this way that the problems and contradictions revealed in Field's social security proposals could be overcome. It is probably fair to say that, when it comes to social security policy, Field has indeed got much by way of insight and analysis to offer. However, his proposals for reform will not make welfare work because the problems which they actually address cannot be solved by the reform of welfare alone.

Despite the crisis in which it can now be found, therefore, welfare is nevertheless an integral part of our complex modern social and economic order. It is for this reason, along with many others, that it cannot simply be abandoned as some on the right might suggest. But it also for this reason that it cannot alone be charged with the burden of recreating effective social protection, whatever the moral basis of this might be. Making welfare work is not a task to be undertaken through welfare reform alone.

Field wants us to focus on self-interest and moral responsibility; but altruism, collectivism and redistribution keep creeping back onto the agenda. He wants us to concentrate on benefit protection and benefit recipients, but labour market priorities and investment strategies play too important a role in determining the real incentives affecting decisions on employment to permit the manipulation of benefits to take place in isolation from other policy changes. Remoralising welfare through self-interest may look like a radical and yet realistic way of making welfare work; but the assumptions behind it are too closed and its frame of reference too tight to provide the solution to the crisis in welfare with which it has been charged.

Notes

1   Field, F., *Losing Out: The Emergence of Britain's Underclass*, Oxford: Blackwell, 1989.

2   Murray, C., *Losing Ground: American Social Policy 1950-1980*, New York: Basic Books, 1984.

3   Green, D.G., *Community Without Politics: A Market Approach to Welfare Reform*, London: IEA Health and Welfare Unit, 1996.

4   Etzioni, A., *The Spirit of Community*, New York: Crown Publishers Inc., 1993.

5   Green, D.G., *op. cit.*, chapter 5.

6   Green, D.G., *op. cit.*

7   Beveridge, Sir W., *Report on Social Insurance and Allied Services*, Cmd. 6404, London: HMSO, 1942.

8   Harris, J., 'The Webbs, the Charity Organisation Society and the Ratan Tata Foundation: Social Policy from the Perspective of 1912' in Bulmer, M., Lewis, J. and Piachaud, D. (eds.), *The Goals of Social Policy*, London:Unwin Hyman, 1989.

9   Field, F., *Making Welfare Work: Reconstructing Welfare for the Millennium*, London: Institute of Community Studies, 1995, chapter 7.

10   Green, D.G., *op. cit.*, chapter 5.

11   Borrie Commission, *Social Justice: Strategies for Renewal - The Report of the Commission on Social Justice*, London: Vintage, 1994.

12   Hills, J., *Changing Tax: How the Tax System Works and How to Change It*, London: Child Poverty Action Group, 1988; see also Hills, J., *The Future of Welfare: A Guide to the Debate*, York: The Joseph Rowntree Foundation, 1993; and Hills, J., *Joseph Rowntree Foundation Inquiry into Income and Wealth*, Vol. 2, York: The Joseph Rowntree Foundation, 1995.

13   Department of Social Security (DSS), *Households Below Average Incomes: A Statistical Analysis 1979-1992/93*, London: HMSO, 1995.

14   Hills, J., *op. cit.*, 1995.

15   See particularly Hutton, W., *The State We're In*, London: Jonathon Cape, 1994.

Welfare and Character

Alan Deacon

ONE of the most striking features of Frank Field's essay is its emphasis upon the link between the rules which determine eligibility to welfare benefits and the behaviour and character of those who receive them. 'The nature of our character', he claims, 'depends in part on the values which welfare fosters'. Above all, he argues for a reduction in the role of means tests within social security. 'Means tests are the cancer within the welfare state, rotting decent values and overwhelming the honesty and dignity of recipients in almost equal proportions'.

The leadership of the Labour Party may not employ the same vivid language as Field, and nor does it share his preoccupation with the effects of means tests. Nevertheless, it has expressed similar anxieties about the influence of welfare on behaviour and about the need to reinforce the responsibilities and obligations of claimants. In a speech in March 1995, for example, Tony Blair spoke of the need to eliminate the 'social evil of welfare dependency amongst able-bodied people'. This, he argued, would require the creation of a society in which all had a stake. Such a society, however, is then able to demand responsibility in return. 'It allows us to be much tougher and hard-headed in the rules we apply and how we apply them'.[1] As examples of what this would involve, Blair cited the introduction of home/school contracts which would set out parents' obligations in respect of 'attendance and time-keeping, homework and standards' and the 'tightening up' by local authorities of 'tenancy agreements to include specific conditions of good behaviour'.

An important influence upon the debate, and particularly upon Tony Blair himself, are the ideas of the Communitarian movement in the United States and its leading advocate Amitai Etzioni. In broad terms, Etzioni's argument is that contemporary western societies are too preoccupied with rights and neglect the obligations which individuals owe to the wider community. Nevertheless, he also places great emphasis upon the importance of character development:

> There is little mystery as to what proper character development entails. In essence, it is acquiring the capacity to control one's impulses and to mobilise oneself for acts other than the satisfaction of biological needs and immediate desires ... Citizens and community members need self-control so that they will not demand ever more services and handouts while being unwilling to pay taxes and make contributions to the commons.[2]

There are three questions which arise immediately and which form the focus of this commentary.

- What do Frank Field and others mean when they use such terms as 'behaviour', 'character', and 'human nature'?
- What explains this apparent preoccupation with the effects of welfare upon behaviour and character amongst politicians and some academic commentators on the centre-left?
- What, if anything, does this new debate about behaviour and character add to our understanding of poverty? Does it reflect real changes in the nature of poverty and deprivation, or is it just another exercise in 'blaming the victim'?

Before attempting to answer these questions, however, it is worth under-lining the significance of the shift which has taken place.

The Orthodoxy of the Centre-Left

For much of the post-war period the debate about the future of welfare on the centre-left of British politics has rested upon a near-consensus that the causes of poverty and deprivation lie in social and economic structures and not in the character or behaviour of poor people themselves. Unemployment, for example, is seen—in Beveridge's classic phrase—as a 'a problem of industry', not of individuals. Personal characteristics may play a part in determining who finds a job and who remains out of work, but the aggregate level of unemployment is determined by economic forces way beyond the control of an individual or group of individuals. Similarly, it is recognised that there may be a disproportionate incidence of mental illness or alcoholism amongst homeless people, but this again only helps to determine who becomes homeless. It is the shortage of suitable and affordable accommodation which makes it inevitable that some people are without a home.

It follows that individual pathologies are seen as the consequences, not the causes, of wider social problems. To condemn the unemployed man or woman who becomes demoralised through repeated rejection, or the alienated youth growing up without hope on sink estates, is to punish people twice over for being born into households at the wrong end of a grossly inequitable distribution of income and wealth.

The implications for policy which follow from such an analysis are clear. If the problems of poverty are rooted in inequitable social structures, then it is futile to try to solve those problems by changing people. If there are not enough jobs, then talk of work incentives or of the workshy is both irrelevant and inhumane. The point was made vividly in a report of the then Supplementary Benefits Commission in 1980:

> To increase incentives while unemployment accelerates upwards is like trying to encourage someone to jump into a swimming pool while the water is drained out.[3]

Similarly, to talk of the duties or obligations of the poor is to suggest that they are in some way responsible for their own condition. The idea that the unemployed, for example, should be compelled to accept work or training in return for benefit must imply that without such a sanction some people will remain out of work unnecessarily: that is, that their unemployment is in some sense voluntary.

Worse still, to talk of the character of the poor is to revive the language of the nineteenth century; and especially the harsh judgementalism of the Charity Organisation Society (COS) with its emphasis upon the need to distinguish between the 'helpable' and the 'unhelpable'. If poor people bear the costs of social changes and of inequalities which benefit the rest of society, the argument runs, then they should be compensated through social policies which meet their needs and treat them with respect. Above all this requires welfare benefits and services which are provided as rights, free of conditions regarding their behaviour and far removed from the intrusive and stigmatising enquiries advocated by the COS and others who have championed the importance of character.

The above outline is inevitably an over-simplification, and one which neglects much recent theorising about the nature of social divisions.[4] Even so, the contrast with Field's indictment of welfare as 'the enemy within' whose rules 'actively undermine the moral fabric of our characters' could scarcely be more stark.[5]

'Character', 'Behaviour' and 'Human Nature'

A central difficulty of Field's work is that he uses these terms almost interchangeably. In fact, the way in which a person behaves is closely linked to his or her character but this does not mean that they are the same thing. Indeed, it is argued here that Field's confusion of behaviour and character is unnecessarily provocative, while his discussion of human nature is incomplete.

Broadly speaking the debate about *behaviour and welfare* is concerned with the extent to which people respond to the incentives and disincentives created by welfare provision. There are very few, for example, who would dispute that labour market activity is affected by the rules governing eligibility for unemployment benefit. A good example—given by Field—is the way in which the benefit rules have contributed to the growing polarisation between households with two earners and those with none. Nevertheless, the issues are often complex, and Eithine McLaughlin has recently outlined the formidable methodological problems in researching them adequately.[6] The important point here, however, is that to pursue one's self-interest in this sense is not seen as blameworthy, it is 'what anyone would do'. Indeed, benefit rules, taxation policies, and systems of pay determination all assume that people will, by and large, act in this way.

The discussion of *character* has long been very different, and focused upon someone's personal qualities and attributes rather than her or his activities. As Collini notes, the Victorians used the term 'to refer to the possession of certain highly-valued moral qualities... The contrast was with behaviour which was random, impulsive, feckless'.[7] This is also the sense in which the term is used by Etzioni who refers to 'the psychological muscles that allow a person to control impulses and defer gratification'.[8] Similarly, James Q. Wilson has criticised economists who assume that values and beliefs can be taken as given and focus solely upon the way in which human behaviour 'changes in response to changes in the costs and benefits of alternative courses of action'. In fact, he argues, some people will not respond in the predicted manner because they do not have the same values, beliefs and habits as everyone else. 'To put it plainly, they lack character'.[9]

The distinction between behaviour and character is not absolute. It is possible, for example, that a widespread change in behaviour may over time affect popular expectations and thereby shape attitudes and character. Indeed, it will be seen later that Charles Murray and others have argued that it is in just such a way that social security benefits have eroded the work ethic and undermined the two-parent family. Nevertheless, the fact remains that there is a crucial difference between character and behaviour. To 'lack character' is seen as blameworthy. It is not just the pursuit of self-interest—'what anyone would do'—but is something which requires and deserves a punitive response. The example of such an response which is often cited is, of course, that of the COS.

It is important to acknowledge at this point that in *Making Welfare Work* and elsewhere Field has been careful to distance himself from at least some aspects of the philosophy of the COS. It is also true, as he argues, that in the late nineteenth century an emphasis upon character was not 'an idiosyncratic concern of the Charity Organisation Society... [but] ... was very much part of working-class culture and aspiration.[10] The fact remains, however, that talk of character and of moral fibre is redolent of the COS and in particular of an uncompromising judgementalism which labelled a *majority* of the poor as an unhelpable 'Residuum'. This, for example, is how they were described in 1895 by one of the Society's leading lights, Helen Dendy (later Helen Bosanquet):

> The Residuum, she asserted, displayed all the defects of character which rendered it industrially incompetent: absence of foresight and self control; recklessness; aimless drifting; self-indulgence; an insuperable aversion to steady work; low intellect; degradation of the natural affections to animal instincts; a disposition unfavourable to the acquisition of skill, and many other vices of similar kinds.[11]

Moreover, the COS was adamant that the task of assisting the minority who were helpable should be undertaken solely by voluntary bodies. Character could only by improved through the discriminating casework of charities, and the Society was resolutely opposed to the payment of insurance benefits as of right. The same preoccupation with the lifestyle of the poor and the same belief in the efficacy of intensive casework can be found in the literature on 'problem families' which was still being published in the 1950s, and which forms an important link between the Residuum of the 1890s and the underclass of the 1980s.[12]

In short, it is argued here that for all the fierceness of his language Field is more concerned with the influence of welfare upon behaviour than he is with the character of the poor as that has been generally understood in the past.

The debate about *human nature* is even more complex and difficult than that about character. As Cowen notes, a 'theory of human nature expresses relationships and underlying assumptions about the world'.[13] Here again, Field can be criticised for overstating the differences between himself and the post-war orthodoxy and paying insufficient attention to the differences between his position and that of other writers who have emphasised the role of character and human nature.

The starting point is that Field can be best understood as a Christian Socialist, an intellectual tradition exemplified for many by the work of Richard Tawney and articulated latterly by academic commentators such as A. H. Halsey and Ronald Preston and politicians such as Tony Blair, his predecessor John Smith and the current shadow spokesman on social security Chris Smith.

As Halsey notes, central to the Christian Socialist tradition 'is the doctrine of personal responsibility under virtually all social circumstances. People act under favourable and unfavourable conditions but remain responsible moral agents'.[14] It is this which underpins Field's rejection of what he sees as the determinism of the post-war orthodoxy and his admiration for the working-class mutual aid movements of the late nineteenth century.

> The responsibility for self improvement was clearly located. It rested with individuals themselves, although it was sought through co-operative effort... The individual was not demeaned as he or she is by much of today's left wing ideology which puts all the emphasis on structural causes as the reasons for preventing personal advance. But neither was it naïve in believing that the structural forces were without importance. Again a proper sense of balancing both these arguments was, I believe, achieved. (p. 40).

The lack a 'proper sense of balance' within the post-war orthodoxy was in turn a reflection of the prevailing assumptions regarding human motivation and behaviour. This can be illustrated most readily by comparing the position of Richard Tawney with that of Richard Titmuss. It is universally acknowledged that Titmuss's ideas dominated academic discussion of social policy for much of the post-war period, and that in his commitment to equality and social integration Titmuss was the spiritual heir of Tawney. That inheritance, however, was incomplete. As Simon Robinson has pointed out, Tawney held a 'Christian view of man as sinful, as well as capable of compassion'. This precluded 'any simple appeal to, or reliance upon, altruism' and led Tawney 'to stress responsibilities and duties rather than rights'.[15] In contrast, Titmuss's 'view of humanity' was 'far more optimistic ... Hence his moralism emphasises the duties of the state to the individual and not the obligations of the individual'.[16]

Similarly Ronald Preston has cited Titmuss as an example of those who:

> have been misled by the utopian element in Tawney's thought (without noting his incidental qualifications) ... This ... has the effect of presenting people of conservative disposition with an entirely unnecessary weapon. They are able to scoff at radicals and socialists as impractical idealists who do not understand the realities of human nature.[17]

It is argued below that it is this which largely explains the non-judgementalism of the Titmuss tradition and its reluctance to engage in debates about incentives or behaviour. It is further argued that it is no coincidence that the challenge to that tradition has come from Christian Socialists such as Field. The crucial point here, however, is that there is not a simple dichotomy between the utopianism of Titmuss and the 'Hobbesian state of affairs' described by Charles Murray. As Field himself argues, there is a balance to be struck. In his eagerness to highlight the limitations of a structural analysis, however, Field has said too little about the patent weaknesses of individualist explanations.

In a penetrating recent essay Lawrence Mead has called for 'a new political language that considers more candidly the questions of human nature that now underlie politics'.[18] He went on to distinguish his 'vision of human nature' from that of Charles Murray and also from that of William Julius Wilson, an American sociologist who places a greater emphasis upon the importance of social structures in explanations of poverty.

> For Murray, poor adults are short-sighted calculators who are tempted into dysfunction by the disincentives of welfare. For Wilson, they are driven into disorder by a changing economy that denies them jobs that could support a family. My own view ... is that they are depressed but dutiful, willing to observe mainstream norms if only government will enforce them. But none of us has defended these premises in enough depth, or linked them clearly enough to our prescriptions.[19]

It is argued here that there is a similar need for Frank Field to set out more fully the premises which underlie the case for 'stakeholder welfare', and, that if he did so, those premises would be less about character than about behaviour.

The Revival of the 'Character' Debate

There is no single explanation for the revival of interest in the relationship between welfare, behaviour and character. It is due in part to the impact upon the British debate of the writings of American conservatives such as Charles Murray and Lawrence Mead; in part to the growing influence of Christian Socialism; in part to changes in the nature and distribution of poverty; in part to the growing polarisation of British society; and in part to the anxieties expressed in all parties about the level of public spending on welfare. All of these factors are inter-related, none would be decisive in the absence of the others, and the relative importance of each will vary considerably from one politician or commentator to another.

Charles Murray's ideas are too familiar to require repetition here. In essence, however, his central argument is that the American War on Poverty not only failed to improve the lot of the poor but made their position much worse. It did this because it changed the welfare system in ways which made 'it profitable for the poor to behave in the short term in ways that were destructive in the long term'.[20] The nature of these perverse incentives was illustrated most starkly by the growth in the number of young, never-married mothers and the precipitate decline in the labour force participation rates of young men. In the first case, the increase in the rates of benefit paid to single mothers, together with the liberalisation of the rules relating to cohabitation, had the effect of greatly increasing the attractiveness of young motherhood compared to low paid work or marriage to a husband on low wage. In the second case, the same benefit changes had the effect of lessening the pressure on young men to work since it was now easier for them to evade financial responsibility for children they had fathered.

Two aspects of Murray's arguments are particularly relevant here. The first is the way in which he has modified his position from one which stressed the rationality of the poor to one which emphasises the links between behaviour and character. In his original book *Losing Ground* Murray argued that:

> poor and not-poor alike, use the same general calculus in arriving at decisions; only the exigencies are different. Poor people play with fewer chips and cannot wait as long for results ... the behaviours that are 'rational' are different at different economic levels.[21]

Critics, however, have pointed out that the link between the rise in the number of single mothers and the generosity of the US welfare system is nothing like as straight forward as Murray suggests. Indeed the real value of the payments made to single mothers actually declined in the 1970s. Murray's response has been to argue that there is a 'threshold' or 'break-even' level of benefit at which it is possible for a young woman to cope as a single mother. 'Once this break point is passed, welfare benefits become an enabling factor: they do not cause single women to decide to have a baby, but they enable women who are pregnant to make the decision to keep the baby'.[22] Above this point further fluctuations in the level of benefit were of little significance. In Britain in 1990 he argued that the 'problem' was that benefits 'enabled many young women to do something they would naturally like to do'.[23] In other words, Murray is claiming that the perverse incentives generated by welfare have a cumulative effect and become self-perpetuating over time. This happens when the values held within low-income communities change, that is when the character of the poor changes. This aspect of Murray's analysis is most evident in his discussion of the erosion of the status of the working poor.

A consistent and important theme of recent conservative writing in the US is the betrayal of the hard working respectable poor by liberal policy making élites. Few have employed this rhetoric more effectively than Murray. Above all, he claims, it was poor parents struggling to maintain their independence and keep their children out of trouble who were undermined by the indiscipline in schools and the crime on the streets which were fostered by the refusal of liberals to judge and condemn.

> It was wrong to take from the most industrious, most responsible poor—take safety, education, justice, status—so that we could cater to the least industrious, least responsible ... The injustice of the policies was compounded by the almost complete immunity of the élite from the price they demanded of the poor.[24]

Most pernicious of all, Murray argues, was the attempt to lessen the stigma attached to receipt of welfare. This had devastating consequences for those who were working in unpleasant jobs which paid little more than benefits, and now saw their relative standing in the community destroyed. In reality the only way out of poverty is to stick at school, get and hold down a job and accept responsibility for yourself and your dependants. Welfare, however, was now being provided as of right to people who had failed to do any of those things. The inevitable effect was to 'withdraw the status reinforcements for upward mobility' and young people in particular would draw the obvious lesson,

> To someone who is not yet persuaded of the satisfactions of making one's own way, there is something laughable about a person who doggedly keeps working at a lousy job for no tangible reason at all. And when working no longer provides either income or status, the last reason for working has truly vanished. The man who keeps working is, in fact, a chump.[25]

In the case of Lawrence Mead the focus on character is clear and unambiguous. Like Murray he believes that the growth in poverty stemmed primarily from the failure of the poor to work. This was not because jobs were not available but because the poor either would not take them or could not keep them. The key problem, he argues, is the lack of competence of the poor. They lack the capacity to fulfil their basic social obligations 'to learn, work, support one's family and respect the rights of others'.[26] The solution was not to withdraw benefits as Murray had proposed but to reform welfare to make it more 'authoritative' and use to it improve the conduct and character of the poor. 'The main problem' he wrote, 'lies not with the poor themselves but with political authorities who refuse to govern them firmly'.[27] The problem hitherto has been that benefits were 'entitlements given regardless of the behaviour of clients'.[28] The answer, then, was to make eligibility for welfare conditional on improved conduct. The most obvious form of such conditionality is so-called 'workfare'—the requirement that the poor work in return for benefits. It is very important to stress, however, that conditionality in the USA goes far beyond this and encompasses such things as school attendance, compliance with immunization requirements, and the imposition of financial sanctions upon families who have further children when already in receipt of welfare.[29]

The impact of these ideas upon the Thatcher governments is well known, but they have also influenced the wider debate. This influence is reflected, not only in the policies now being proposed by 'New Labour', but in the language in which such policies are being justified. Labour's 'welfare to work' scheme, for example, would withdraw unemployment benefits from young people who do not agree to participate in work or training programmes. This has been defended in forthright terms by Peter Mandelson and Roger Liddle, two of Tony Blair's closest allies:

> Such a tough discipline is necessary to ... break the culture of hopelessness, idleness and cynicism which a concentration of hard-core unemployment has bred in the many estates throughout Britain where a generation has been brought up on the dole.[30]

Similarly there is little sign of the 'liberal betrayal' castigated by Murray in Mandelson and Liddle's insistence that 'New Labour stands for the ordinary families who work hard and play by the rules' and that 'New Labour's enemies' include 'the irresponsible who fall down on their obligations to their families and therefore their community'.[31]

It was stressed earlier, however, that the influence of Murray and Mead upon the centre-left cannot be seen in isolation from that of communitarianism or the growing importance of Christian Socialism. A further and very important factor has been the way in which at least part of their analysis appears to have been vindicated by the changing pattern of poverty in Britain.

This is especially true of Frank Field, whose position derives in large part from his perception of what is happening 'on the ground'. In *Making Welfare Work*, for example, he recounts how, as early as 1981, he was told by a group of women in his constituency of Birkenhead that the introduction of the then family income supplement and more generous rent rebates made it possible for them to support themselves and their children out of their own wage. In consequence 'they had got rid of the 'jerk' to whom they had been married'.

> The break up agreement was that the men would leave, no maintenance would be demanded, but, in return, the leaving had to be complete, with fathers having no continuing access to the children. All the women I spoke to that day expressed satisfaction with the arrangement. The children were not there to ask whether they viewed events so calmly.[32]

As Field notes, single parenthood is now the major cause of child poverty—and 'we do not know the long-term effects for the 2.3 million children currently living without two parents'.[33] Nevertheless, it is the increase in the number of never-married mothers from 90,000 in 1971 to 490,000 in 1992 which has done more than anything else to highlight the relationship between benefits and behaviour. It is widely believed that on average children in such families suffer considerable disadvantages compared to those living with both parents. Moreover, it is also believed that at least some young women are choosing to become mothers on benefit rather than live with the father of their child or their own parents, and rather than accept whatever employment is available to them. As Mann and Roseneil note:

> These young women are not necessarily 'abandoned' by the fathers, nor should their pregnancies be assumed to be 'accidents'; in this respect, they are not victims.[34]

Mann and Roseneil go on to document the 'moral panic' which this has engendered far beyond the confines of the traditional defenders of family values or morality. Perhaps the clearest example is the response of A.H. Halsey, who told *The Guardian* in February 1993 that 'the decline of the nuclear family is not merely at the root of many social evils but is the cancer in the lungs of the modern left.'

The extent to which the growth in the number of such families has had adverse consequences for the children involved is a complex issue which cannot be resolved here.[35] What matters for the present argument is that many commentators are convinced that this is so, and many of them are also persuaded that the decline of the two-parent family owes at least something to the tax and benefits system.[36] Almost everyone agrees, however, that it would be wrong to take steps which would worsen further the position of children who are already in one-parent families. The result is a conundrum which has generated far more heat than light but which has done much to push the issue of the interaction between benefits, behaviour and character to the forefront of the debate.

Field's proposal that income support should be converted from a passive to a pro-active agency reflects an important shift in perceptions as to what may be reasonably demanded of claimants. Broadly speaking, there has been a growing acceptance that the long-term unemployed are becoming more isolated from the labour market, and that the effects of this isolation are compounded by the demoralisation and loss of self-esteem which follows prolonged joblessness. These are not new fears. In the 1940s they were expressed very powerfully by Christian writers such as William Temple, and also lead Beveridge to propose that after six months benefits should become conditional upon attendance at a work or training centre.[37] In recent years, however, economists such as Richard Layard and Dennis Snower have proposed that the long-term unemployed be offered some form of guarantee of work or training in return for which they would be required to take such opportunities or forgo benefit. They argue that there is a powerful economic justification for this kind of scheme because it improves the supply of labour and thereby the terms of the trade-off between unemployment and inflation.[38] Field himself has argued elsewhere that training should remain voluntary but that fraud should be tackled through a separate package of measures, including a requirement that employers notify the public employment service of all vacancies and a provision that claimants suspected of working and signing be asked to register for work at least once each day.[39]

The revival of interest in character, then, needs to be seen in the context of changes in the form and incidence of poverty, but it should also be located within a wider societal framework. In particular it must be recognised that the debate is taking place within an increasingly divided and polarised society, and at a time when politicians in all the major parties are becoming more and more anxious about the level of public expenditure on welfare.

The position regarding the growth of inequality in Britain is well known and the details will not be rehearsed here. According to the official statistics on 'Households Below Average Incomes' (HBAI), the richest tenth of households enjoyed an increase in real income (after housing costs) of 62 per cent between 1979 and 1992/3, compared with a rise of 38 per cent for the population as a whole and a decline of 17 per cent for the poorest tenth. It is true that the accuracy of this HBAI data has been challenged,[40] but few people dispute that the gap between rich and poor has widened. Indeed Peter Lilley has observed that the 'growing dispersion of earning power' is 'the single most significant social change affecting the UK'.[41] What this dispersion means for poor families has been spelt out in recent research for the Joseph Rowntree Foundation.[42] Such inequalities not only threaten social cohesion: they create a level of ignorance about the realities of poverty which in turn provides a fertile environment for ideas about the emergence of a 'new rabble'.[43]

Much the same can be said about the widespread anxiety concerning the costs of welfare. There is scarcely an aspect of the social security system which is not being subjected to a fundamental review within both Whitehall and the opposition parties. Indeed, such is the general eagerness to think the unthinkable that the only option which seems to be definitely ruled out is the retention of the status quo. Such a climate of opinion is clearly more conducive to a thorough reappraisal of the effects of welfare than any since the Second World War. The question, however, is whether the debate is taking social policy in the right direction.

What has Field added to the Debate?

Frank Field has made an enormous contribution to the debate about the future of welfare. He has done so because his focus on the links between benefits and behaviour helps to fill a vacuum in that debate. It was noted earlier that the dominant tradition in academic social policy effectively eschewed discussion of incentives and obligations. In consequence academic and political debates on the left neglected the very issues which were highlighted so dramatically by writers such as Murray and Mead. This in turn meant that the centre-left was more vulnerable than it need have been to the revival of individualist ideas.[44]

Kirk Mann has made similar points regarding the neglect of agency within sociological accounts of poverty. He contends that those who have been most hostile to the idea of an underclass have emphasised the structural causes of poverty and in so doing tended to portray the poor 'as passive victims incapable or unable to make any meaningful decisions'. This is:

> deterministic and may conceal some significant social changes. One of the most obvious examples of how constrained choices are made is the growth in lone mothers claiming benefit ... It is perhaps a banal point to emphasise but, because this change in social behaviour can find no place in dominant accounts of poverty, it has provided commentators like Murray with a space they can fill with more mischievous accounts.[45]

Not only does Field's work occupy this 'space', but he uses the language of Murray to condemn the expansion of means testing which took place under Mrs Thatcher and to call for an expansion of inclusive social insurance. There is a danger, however, that commentators on the centre-left will be distracted from the significance of Field's proposals by the ferocity of his language about 'character'. That danger is exacerbated by the relish with which he attacks the past orthodoxy of his own party. The 'appropriate balance' which he seeks requires him to be equally critical of individualist arguments. The fact is that Murray and Mead are brilliant polemicists who raise important and often uncomfortable questions about the consequences of welfare. Their analyses, however, focus upon the response of individuals to changes in welfare to the exclusion of everything else. They have nothing to say about the fundamental changes now taking place in the labour market such as the growth of part-time and insecure employment nor about the 'growing dispersion of earning power' observed by Peter Lilley.

In short, the value of Frank Field's work is the way in which he has highlighted some crucial and long neglected issues about welfare and behaviour. It would be very unfortunate if those points were lost in the furore created by his misleading and inappropriate references to character.

Notes

1 Blair, T., 'The Rights We Enjoy Reflect The Duties We Owe', Lecture, unpublished, 22 March 1995, pp. 2,7.

2 Etzioni, A., *The Spirit of Community*, New York: Crown Publishers Inc., 1993, p. 90.

3 Supplementary Benefits Commission, *Annual Report for 1979*, Comnd 8033, London: HMSO, 1980, p. 41.

4 See Williams, F., 'New Thinking on Social Policy Research into Inequality, Social Exclusion and Poverty' in Millar, J. and Bradshaw, J. (eds.), *Social Welfare Systems: Towards a New Research Agenda*, University of Bath, 1986.

5 Field, F., *Making Welfare Work*, London: Institute of Community Studies, 1995, pp. 129-30.

6 McLaughlin, E., 'Researching the Behavioural Effects of Welfare Systems' in Millar, J. and Bradshaw, J. (eds.), *Social Welfare Systems: Towards a New Research Agenda*, University of Bath, 1996.

7 Collini, S., 'The Idea of "Character" in Victorian Thought', *Transactions of the Royal Historical Society*, Vol. 35, 1985, pp. 33-34.

8 Etzioni, A., *op. cit.*, p. 91.

9 Wilson, J.Q., 'The Rediscovery of Character: Private Virtue and Public Behaviour', *Public Interest*, Vol. 81, 1985, p. 5.

10 Field, F., *Making Welfare Work, op. cit.*, p. 15.

11 McBriar, A.M., *An Edwardian Mixed Doubles*, Oxford: Clarendon Press, 1987, p. 124.

12 Macnicol, J., 'From Problem Family to Underclass', unpublished paper to the Institute of Contemporary British History Conference, July 1995.

13 Cowen, H., *The Human Nature Debate*, London: Pluto Press, 1994, p. 1.

14 Halsey, A.H., Foreword to Dennis, N. and Erdos, G., *Families Without Fatherhood*, London: IEA Health and Welfare Unit, 1992, p. 1992, p. xi.

15 Robinson, S., 'Tawney's Theory of Equality', unpublished PhD. thesis, University of Edinburgh, 1989, pp.190, 199, 214.

16 *Ibid.*, p.190.

17 Preston, R., *Religion and the Persistence of Capitalism*, London: SCM Press, 1979, p. 109.

18 Mead, L., 'The New Politics of the New Poverty', *Public Interest*, Vol. 103 1992, p. 19.

19 *Ibid.*, pp. 19-20.

20 Murray, C., *Losing Ground: American Social Policy 1950-1980*, New York: Basic Books, 1984, p. 9.

21 *Ibid.*, p. 155.

22 Murray, C., 'Have the Poor Been "Losing Ground"?', *Political Science Quarterly*, Vol. 100, No. 3, 1985, p. 441.

23 Murray, C., *The Emerging British Underclass*, London: IEA Health and Welfare Unit, 1990, p. 30.

24 Murray, C., *Losing Ground, op. cit.*, p. 219.

25 *Ibid.*, p. 185.

26 Mead, L., *Beyond Entitlement: The Social Obligations of Citizenship*, New York: Free Press, 1986, p. 6.

27 *Ibid.*, p. 248.

28 *Ibid.*, p. 65.

29 Wiseman, M., 'Welfare Reform in the States: The Bush Legacy', *Focus*, Vol. 15, 1993.

30 Mandelson, P. and Liddle, R., *The Blair Revolution: Can New Labour Deliver?*, London: Faber and Faber, 1996, p. 102.

31 *Ibid.*, pp. 18, 20.

32 Field, F., *Making Welfare Work, op. cit.*, p. 11.

33 *Ibid.*, p. 21.

34 Mann, K. and Roseneil, S., 'Some Mothers do 'ave 'em: Backlash and the Gender Politics of the Underclass Debate', *Journal of Gender Studies*, Vol. 3, No. 3, 1994, p. 321.

35 See Burghes, L., *Lone Parenthood and Family Disruption: The Outcomes for Children*, York: Joseph Rowntree Foundation, 1994.

36 See Morgan, P., *Farewell to the Family?*, IEA Health and Welfare Unit, 1995; and Mandelson, P. and Liddle, R., *op. cit.*, 1996.

37 See Deacon, A., 'Justifying "Workfare": the Historical Context of the "Workfare" Debate' in White, M., (ed.), *Unemployment and Public Policy in a Changing Labour Market*, London: Policy Studies Institute, 1994.

38 Employment Committee, *Second Report: The Right to Work / Workfare*, Session 1995/96, HC 82, London: HMSO, 1996.

39 Field, F. and Owen, M., *Beyond Punishment: Hard Choices on the Road to Full Employability*, London: Institute of Community Studies, 1994.

40 Pryke, R., *Taking the Measure of Poverty*, London: Institute of Economic Affairs, 1995.

41 Quoted in Field, F.,*Making Welfare Work, op. cit.*, p.106.

42 Kempson, E., *Life on a Low Income*, York: Joseph Rowntree Foundation, 1996.

43 Murray, C., *Losing Ground, op. cit.*

44 See Deacon, A., 'Re-reading Titmuss: Moralism, Work and Welfare', *University of Leeds Review*, Vol. 36, 1993, p. 96.

45 Mann, K., *The Secret Agents Within the Underclass: Critical Reflections on Some Recent Theories of Poverty*, Centre for Social Differentiation and Integration, Copenhagen, 1995, p. 35.

Welfare and Civil Society

David G. Green

Introduction

FRANK Field is at the cutting edge of the emerging new socialism and offers four main challenges to prevailing assumptions. First, he opposes the use of the political system to engineer material equality for its own sake, though he does not recoil from all redistribution:

> There is no general groundswell amongst middle-class groups for redistribution of wealth to the poor, particularly in the aftermath of the Thatcher years. Politicians who maintain otherwise are a public menace distracting from the real task.[1]

His second departure is the rehabilitation of self-interest. Welfare, he says, should respect the 'pivotal role' of self-interest and the objective of public policy should be to discover how to satisfy it in ways that serve the common good (above, p. 9). Field's attitude is very different from the conventional socialist view that self-interest is merely another name for selfishness and that any sympathy for self-interest implies support for capitalism, the name for a social order in which the rich exploit the poor. The typical socialist stance has been to contrast the self and the collectivity and to claim that our actions can either take into account our purely private interests or those of others, not both. Concern for the self rules out concern for others and, therefore, to speak of harnessing self-interest in the service of the common interest is self-contradictory. Field's approach is a flat rejection of this doctrine.

Third, he challenges socialist determinism, though he retains strong deterministic assumptions, as I will argue below. The typical socialist standpoint has been that the poor are victims of 'the system'. This view continues to be central to the writings of groups such as the Child Poverty Action Group, whose authors typically regard any attribution of personal responsibility as 'blaming the victim'. For them, social problems can best be resolved by political reform of the system, not directing attention to individual responsibility. To focus on the individual is to scapegoat the poor and divert attention from the real, underlying causes. Judgment-alism should be avoided at all costs. Field's claim that avoidance of stigma is 'no longer the main issue' (above, p. 11) is a direct attack on this belief. Having rejected determinism, Field recognises that worthy ideals need to be held up for individuals to pursue and he goes on to rehabilitate discussion of 'character' and self-improvement.[2]

Fourth, and closely related to their deterministic view that human behaviour is the result of 'outside forces', socialists have also been paternalistic, holding that most people should have their main affairs managed for them by the authorities. This paternalism was unashamed in the earlier part of the century, reflected in the thought of the Webbs. However, during the 1970s and 1980s, a contradictory tendency developed as many on the left took up the libertarian cry for 'choice of lifestyle'. A demand for choice assumes a certain competence on the part of the choosers. If the political authorities are to manage the most important welfare concerns—provision for interruption of earnings through illness, loss of job or old age—then the underlying assumption is that people are *not* competent to do it for themselves. Yet, they are considered competent to choose their lifestyle. This contradiction has been pointed out by Samuel Brittan since the 1960s,[3] and more recently by 'ethical socialists'. They remind the libertarian left of the philosophical assumption of socialists like Tawney, that individuals are personally responsible in all circumstances, even when the circumstances are not of their making. Field belongs to this tradition, and assumes that people are more competent for self-management than has been the socialist norm, though there is still a residual paternalism exemplified by his demand for pension contributions to be made compulsory for all.

I will turn now to his specific proposals: first, the reform of social security for those out of work but able to work.

Out of Work and Fit for Work

There are three main traditions of thought about assistance for the able-bodied poor. The first is concerned to devise tax/benefit systems that create incentives to work. The second is concerned less about incentives to work and more about redistribution from rich to poor. The third tradition rejects redistribution for its own sake and asserts that no benefit system *alone* can ever design material incentives sufficient to encourage every person to work. Instead, we must look to a sense of freely-accepted duty, taught and fostered by the fundamental institutions of a free society, including the family and the voluntary associations that make up our common life. Field belongs to the first tradition and my criticism to the third. The 'incentives' and 'duty' traditions are not mutually exclusive, but the champions of duty assert that—whilst prudent public policies are an indispensable part of the remedy—no amount of designing and redesigning benefit systems will ever be decisive on its own.

Within the 'incentives' tradition three main approaches can be discerned: first, means testing (or targeting); second, guaranteed income financed from national insurance contributions; and third, guaranteed income financed from general taxes without any pretext that insurance 'premiums' have been paid. Field opposes means testing and advocates guaranteed income deemed to be based on national insurance. I will argue that he expects too much from national insurance and that, on the evidence of similar schemes elsewhere, his proposals will not achieve the expected results.

Field's claim is that abstention from work, reduced saving by the poor and benefit fraud are the result of means tests. He hypothesises that, if means tests were replaced by payments of guaranteed benefit funded by national insurance contributions, these types of behaviour would be reduced or eliminated.

My counter claim is that abstention from work, reduced work effort, lower saving and benefit fraud are not *only* the result of the benefit system, though it plays a part; and more particularly, I argue that they are not *only* the result of means testing, though it makes matters worse in some respects. Human behaviour is not only the result of 'incentives' or 'outside forces'. We often face conscious choices and, no less important, we are capable of internalising rules of behaviour, thinking or unthinking, which make human co-operation possible. Our capacity to adopt moral virtues as our own cannot be satisfactorily understood if we confine ourselves to the language of incentives. It certainly has much to do with the mechanisms by which we signal to one another our approval or disapproval of kinds of conduct, but the benefit system is one and only one of the many institutions through which such messages are conveyed. Reforming benefits alone cannot restore a sense of duty to work or deter fraud. We must also renew our understanding of the institutions that uphold shared moral standards and encourage the best in people. To direct attention to the 'inner person' is not an exercise in scapegoating or distraction from underlying factors; it is to direct attention to one of the most important real, underlying causes.

Field's strictures about character show that he is close to understanding the importance of upholding a cultural ideal across the generations, but unfortunately he has not seen that his pre-occupation with national insurance through 'stakeholder' corporations will make matters worse by crowding out the voluntary associations that, until very recently, were central to the maintenance of a shared sense of duty to others.

Means Testing

Means testing, according to Field, is recruiting a nation of cheats and liars and responsibility lies 'primarily' with politicians who support the existence and extension of means-tested welfare (above, p. 11).

The Conservatives have increased means testing of some benefits. Family Income Supplement (now Family Credit), Housing Benefit, and rate rebates (now Council Tax Benefit) were previously income, but not means, tested. From 1988 they were available only when both income and capital fell below a certain point. Work is discouraged, says Field, because as income rises benefits fall; saving is penalised because having savings creates ineligibility; and means tests tax honesty, where honesty disqualifies (above, p. 11).

The Government, says Field, is naïve about how human motivation responds to incentives and disincentives (above, p. 15). And he calls for a realistic view of human nature: 'Self-interest, not altruism, is mankind's main driving force' (above, p. 19). Instead of means testing he wishes to restore the Beveridge ideal of most people relying on insurance benefits for which they have paid, so that when earnings are interrupted through unemployment they will have a small but guaranteed income on which to build. He shows how, since Beveridge's time, fewer and fewer unemployed people have been eligible for unemployment benefit. In 1951, 67 per cent were eligible, whereas by 1994 it was only 17 per cent.[4] Adequacy of benefits is not the problem, he says, but non-payment of contributions,[5] and his remedy is to relax contribution requirements so that benefit is payable after 13 weeks in work.

But here is the first weakness in his argument. There is a lingering determinism in the explanation he offers. Field assumes that reduced work effort is the result of benefit 'traps'. If people are financially better off out of work than in, they are in the unemployment trap. And if they are on low pay, and lose in withdrawn benefits 80-100 per cent of each additional pound earned from work, they are in the poverty trap. In these circumstances it is expected that people will not work at all or work less. Field believes that, if the contribution requirements were less demanding, then more people would qualify for national insurance benefits, receive a guaranteed income when out of work, and would not be deterred from finding a new job or increasing their hours of work.

A preliminary objection to his argument is that, whilst means testing may produce the poverty trap, it does not single-handedly create the unemployment trap. It is the payment of a benefit for not working, whether means tested or not, that gives people the option of refraining from work. As Professor Layard argued in his recent evidence to the House of Commons Employment Committee, international comparisons reveal a correlation between the length of time benefit can be claimed and the duration of long-term unemployment. In countries with no time limit there is more long-term unemployment.[6] Means testing, however, does reduce the attraction of earning small amounts of extra money and can discourage a partner from taking a part-time job, since all but £5 (£15 if unemployed for two years or more) would be deducted from income support payments.[7]

But the more fundamental objection is that Field operates with an incomplete view of human nature. He is operating on the assumption that human behaviour can be understood as a series of reactions to 'outside forces'. Thus, the benefit system creates 'incentives', that is, it makes some kinds of behaviour more advantageous than others and people react accordingly. The defect in the argument is that not everyone reacts in the same way to similar incentives. That is, human values or virtues are 'variables' independent of the benefit system. Field coined the term 'poverty trap', to describe the position up to 1982, when it was possible to lose more than 100 per cent of each additional pound earned because of the withdrawal of benefits.[8] Since 1982, reforms have meant that no one loses more than 100 per cent, but benefit withdrawal still means an effective marginal tax rate of 80-90 per cent for part of the income range. According to the April 1995 Tax/Benefit Model Tables, a married couple with two children aged four and six on income support would always be better off in work with earnings of £75 a week upwards. However, the rate at which benefits are withdrawn would leave them with an effective marginal tax rate of over 90 per cent until earnings reached about £200 a week. At £225 per week the rate is 85 per cent and at £250, 76 per cent.[9]

Not everyone, however, reacts to this situation by refraining from work altogether or reducing work effort. Some work out of sheer self-respect, or a sense of duty to their family, or to set an example for their children. Others may calculate that it may not be worth earning a little bit more, but that it is worth earning substantially more, either by working significantly longer hours, taking a second job or, more commonly, the second parent taking a job. Small changes in earnings, such as the odd hour of overtime, which lead to 80-90 per cent effective marginal tax rates are not financially attractive, but taking an additional part-time job will often put a family clear of the high-tax zone.

American evidence suggests that this is exactly what does happen in well-motivated, responsible families. One of the weaknesses of studies that emphasise the importance of 'traps' in determining behaviour is that they look only at the impact on individuals receiving the lowest incomes. They rarely ask whether other people have reacted differently to the incentives and avoided poverty precisely because of their behaviour. For example, Lawrence Mead shows that, in America, there is a significant difference between the work effort of the poor and the non-poor. Many of the non-poor escape poverty only by working harder. Drawing on a study of people below the federal poverty line, he compares 1959, 1975 and 1989 and notes that since the 1960s work effort among the poor in America has dropped sharply.[10]

In 1959, 67.5 per cent of heads of families below the federal poverty line worked at some time during the year. By 1989 the figure had fallen to 48.9 per cent. Those who had worked full time for the whole year fell from 31.5 per cent to 16.2 per cent and those who had done no work at all *increased* from 30.5 per cent to 50.8 per cent. The biggest change was found among heads of families other than single females. Those doing work of some kind fell from 74.9 per cent to 56.8 per cent; those working full-year, full-time from 37.6 per cent to 24.1 per cent; and non-work increased from 22.5 per cent to 42.6 per cent. Mead concludes that reduced work effort explains why many fell below the poverty line. Had they worked harder, as others did, they would not have been poor.[11]

Mead also looks at work effort by the poor, using a relative definition of poverty. He compares the bottom quintile of earners with the top quintile and measures hours of work using a single figure representing the full-year, full-time equivalent. This allows a comparison based on a single figure representing both the number of hours worked and the number of family members in work. In 1970, in families with children, an average of 1.23 adults in the top quintile worked, whereas in the bottom quintile the figure was 0.42.

Comparing 1970 and 1986 Mead found that bottom-quintile families with children reduced work effort from 0.42 to 0.27. The top quintile figure increased slightly from 1.23 to 1.25. Work effort by married couples in the top quintile increased from 1.31 to 1.45, whilst that for married couples in the bottom quintile fell slightly from 0.63 to 0.61, so that in 1986 work effort by the top quintile was more than double that of the bottom quintile. As Mead remarks, 'These work differences go far to explain the radical income differences among families at the top and the bottom of society'.[12]

The reasons typically given for non-work did not apply, says Mead. There were ample jobs available, with new jobs being created from the 1960s to the 1980s. Employment grew 20 per cent in the 1960s, 26 per cent in the 1970s and 19 per cent in the 1980s. Over the 30-year period the labour force grew by 55 million people.[13] There was also no lack of childcare. Workfare programmes made childcare available in ample amounts, but it was not taken up. The Massachusetts Employment and Training Choices program (ET) funded childcare for workfare more generously than any other state and found that only 14 per cent of participants asked for care from the programme. In San Diego, where strenuous efforts were made to secure 100 per cent participation, only 12 per cent claimed reimbursement for childcare costs.[14]

How do the US findings compare with Britain? We can also look at the work effort of the lowest quintile using the series produced by the Institute for Fiscal Studies from 1961, based on the Family Expenditure Survey (see Table 1 p. 92). These figures do not allow an exact comparison, because the measures of work effort are more rudimentary. However, they reveal a similar pattern: a major explanation of the difference between the incomes of the poorest 20 per cent and the non-poor is that the non-poor households have more working members.

In 1961, 5.73 per cent of households in the bottom quintile were individuals in full-time work or couples both of whom were in full-time work. In 1991 the figure had fallen to 1.54 per cent. Similarly, couples with one partner working full time and the other part time comprised 5.84 per cent in 1961, and only 1.73 per cent in 1991. Households with the head unemployed comprised 2.34 per cent in 1961 and 20.06 per cent in 1991.

Information direct from the 1995 Family Expenditure Survey shows a similar picture. Households in higher deciles contain more people working than those in lower deciles, and it is likely that many households in the fourth, fifth and sixth deciles escape poverty because of their greater work effort, as Table 2 (p. 93) suggests.

A pure 'victim' explanation would assert that work effort in lower deciles was lower because no jobs were available and, however hard they tried, the poorest people could not find work. Few argue that extreme case and, in any event, Frank Field does not. He claims that the reduced work effort is the result of perverse incentives resulting from means testing. But as the American evidence shows most clearly, not everyone reacts to the 'incentives' in the same way. Some families would be below the poverty line if the main breadwinner worked fewer hours or if they relied on one income alone. They avoid low total earnings because both partners work. That is, they break out of the poverty trap because the solidarity of the family allows members to work hard in more than one job.

A British study by Harkness, Machin and Waldfogel supports this conclusion. It is based on evidence from the General Household Survey (GHS) and three cross-sectional surveys, the Women and Employment Survey (1980), the British Social Attitudes Survey (an annual survey carried out since 1983), and the British Household Panel Survey (1991).

The Women and Employment Survey questioned 5,588 women aged 16-59, 63 per cent of whom were working full time or part time. The interviewers were trying to discover whether female earnings were peripheral or fundamental to the family's finances. In answer to the statement, 'I couldn't manage unless I was earning', 43 per cent said it was 'definitely true' and a further 27 per cent that it was 'partly true'. Thirty-five per cent said they worked because they needed 'money for basic essentials such as food, rent or mortgage' and 20 per cent to 'earn money to buy extras'. The next most important reasons were 'to earn money of my own' (14 per cent) and 'for the company of other people' (seven per cent).[15]

The British Social Attitudes Survey asked questions about reasons for work in 1984 and 1991. The most frequent response was that married women worked to earn money for 'essentials'. In 1984, 46 per cent of married working women stated that their main reason for working was for money to buy 'essentials', while the comparable figure in 1991 was 43 per cent.[16]

The British Household Panel Survey produced similar findings: 42 per cent said that their main reason for working was to earn money for 'essentials', compared with 14 per cent who said that it was to earn money for 'extras'.[17]

Evidence from the General Household Survey shows that employment rates between 1979-81 and 1989-91 rose most for middle-income families, and that families in the two lowest deciles reduced their employment rates (primarily because of the increase in families headed by a single woman).[18] Harkness and her colleagues also compare families headed by a married or cohabiting couple with those headed by a lone female. In families headed by a couple, women in the second to fifth income deciles increased their employment rates between 1979-81 and 1989-91, whilst the rate of increase for women in higher-earning families was slower.[19] This evidence suggests that some families threatened by low incomes responded by increasing their work effort, and that their additional work effort explains why they were not in poverty when others were.

Harkness and her colleagues then asked how many families would be in poverty were it not for women's earnings. They deployed a relative definition of poverty (half average equivalised household income as reported by the Households Below Average Income [HBAI] series of reports). Eight per cent of married and cohabiting couples were poor in 1989-91. If the women had earned nothing, and the men had not changed the number of hours they worked in response to falling family income, then 12 per cent of families would have been poor.[20]

Thus, there is substantial evidence from a variety of sources that sticking together as a family so that both partners can work is an effective strategy for escaping poverty, and one that is followed by many households. This strategy is especially prevalent among some ethnic minorities, such as families of Indian origin. Some of those in lower income deciles could also escape low income if they adopted the same approach.

To sum up: so far I have argued that poverty cannot be explained purely as a reaction to the benefit system. Some people faced with the very same incentives react differently and escape poverty because of their determination to work harder.

Benefits Without Means Tests

But there is also further evidence to refute Field's claim that the replacement of means testing will reduce unemployment. His alternative of a guaranteed income without means testing has already been tried and found also to be associated with reduced work effort.

Various efforts have been made in America to create a universal entitlement to benefits without value judgement. During the 1960s and 1970s tax credit or negative income tax (NIT) schemes were widely advocated and the idea was subjected to rigorous experimental testing in the 1970s.

The largest-scale income maintenance experiments were conducted in Seattle and Denver from 1970 to 1978. They included 4,800 families, more than all the other NIT experiments put together. Different rates of guaranteed income were tested: the lowest guaranteed payment was 95 per cent of the US poverty line, and the highest 140 per cent, with an intermediate level of 120 per cent. Different tax rates, varying from 50 per cent to 70 per cent of additional earnings above the guaranteed income, were also tested. All participating families were compared with a control group receiving normal income-tested welfare benefits (mainly Aid to Families with Dependent Children and Food Stamps).[21]

The experiment allows us to test the effect on work effort of making a no-strings payment that is neither income nor means (savings) tested. The experiments resemble Field's scheme in that they provide a guaranteed income in or out of work, although they were not financed by national insurance contributions. The Seattle and Denver (SIME/DIME) experiments meant that it was more worthwhile than in Britain for a second partner to take a job. Under Britain's income support system all but £10 (£15 for those unemployed two years or more) of a couple's additional earnings would be deducted from benefit, whereas under the NIT schemes work by one or more family members yielding income above the guaranteed level always produced additional earnings. Savings were not taken into account. The 'unemployment trap' remained, as it would under Field's scheme, for those families who could not earn more than the benefit level, but the 'poverty trap' was diminished compared with Britain by applying tax rates on additional earnings above the guaranteed income of no more than 70 per cent.

Contrary to initial expectations, the experiments found, not only that work effort was reduced, but also that NIT appeared to increase the rate of marital dissolution.[22] Robins, Tuma and Yaeger report the effects on work effort as follows. NIT payments significantly increased the length of spells of unemployment by an average of 9.4 weeks (27 per cent) for husbands; 50 weeks (42 per cent) for wives; and 56 weeks (60 per cent) for single female heads of families. The length of periods in work was also significantly reduced by 24 weeks (13 per cent) for husbands and 23 weeks (15 per cent) for single female heads.[23]

Researchers also looked at hours of work per week and found that reductions were concentrated in non-heads of families. Males who remained non-heads of families during the study reduced their hours of work per week by 43 per cent. Males who became heads of families during the study reduced by 33 per cent on average. Females who remained non-heads reduced by 42 per cent, but there was no response by males and females who became 'unrelated individuals' or females who married. The reduced work effort is not accounted for by increased education.[24]

To sum up: the SIME/DIME experiment compared recipients of guaranteed income with a control group receiving normal income-tested benefits (Aid to Families with Dependent Children and Food Stamps). It discovered a reduction in work effort by recipients of guaranteed benefit payments. This experience refutes Field's claim that means testing (including income testing and capital testing), rather than the payment of a guaranteed income, is *solely* responsible. It also shows that some benefit systems have stronger work-reducing effects than others.

Thus, two propositions are being asserted. First, the payment of a cash benefit regardless of work effort will not overcome the work-reducing effects of means testing. Second, 'the culture' is an independent variable. Work effort is not *wholly* determined by the welfare system, though it is influenced by it and some benefit systems have a bigger effect than others.

Culture as an Independent Variable

If it is true that values, virtues, habits and dispositions are independent of the benefit system, we should seek to restore the vitality of the institutions that mould virtues, rather than concentrate solely on reform of the mechanics of the system alone. Here we touch upon a philosophical dispute about human nature. Are people best understood as 'cash registers' reacting to incentives, or are they bearers of a moral compass who may or may not attach much weight to material advantage?[25] And if the latter, how is virtue encouraged? Field accepts that desirable virtues are not promoted at present, but would his proposals be an improvement?

A particular difficulty is that national insurance, on which he places strong reliance, played a part historically in destroying mutual aid societies, which had helped to mould the personal virtues on which a free society rests (and that the national insurance scheme took for granted). In the 1940s the mood was in favour of the convenience of one national insurance payment, but the price was the eradication of the fundamental character-building institutions that pre-dated national insurance, as Beveridge himself regretted later. This is how Beveridge voiced his plea to preserve a role for friendly societies in *The Times* on 5 February 1946. The Friendly Societies:

> should be allowed to do the local personal work for their own members in the interests of those members. To admit this plea may make the administrative task of a few officials slightly more complicated. But it will make things better and simpler for the consumer of insurance. *To reject this plea now and set up an all-embracing State machine will be final. To admit it will leave room for experiment and trial.* There is no reason for doubting the care and skill of the Friendly Societies, but if it should be proved by experience that the agency plan involves trouble out of proportion to its benefits it can be abandoned after trial. *It should not be rejected without trial, for none of the reasons given against it hitherto will stand examination.* (Italics in original.)

Beveridge's demand was modest in the extreme, but it was rejected 'without trial' all the same. The problem can be traced back to the 1911 National Insurance Act. Before the Act, friendly societies were providing benefits for over three-quarters of the working population, but they were partially nationalised as 'approved societies' under the Act. Beveridge acknowledged that, even after more than 30 years as approved societies, the friendly societies had retained many of the qualities that made them admirable. He particularly wanted to preserve the personal service to members that was provided over and above any strict entitlement to benefit, not least the regular visiting of the sick or injured and the care provided for elderly members. In addition to providing services, the friendly societies also sought to bring out the best in people, teaching social co-operation, democratic skills, and encouraging an ethos of service.[26] It is not possible to envisage the restoration of a role for such organisations in the face of what Beveridge called (above) 'an all-embracing State machine'.

To sum up: Field's emphasis on national insurance will be counter productive. It will continue to crowd out the emergence of voluntary associations that historically discharged the immediate task of providing benefits more effectively than the state, and also played a vital part in strengthening civil society, by dispersing know-how and commitment, providing opportunities for the service of others and encouraging the best in people. Field has supported an increased role for friendly societies in some of his writings, but they would be little more than sub-contractors under the wing of the state. Such an arrangement would not allow them to discharge the educational task that was historically theirs.

Lessons from Workfare

It has proved possible elsewhere to devise benefit systems that do less harm than the present British system. Field's proposals, however, do not learn the lessons of the most successful overseas schemes, especially US workfare schemes that *require* work. He goes a long way in that direction, but recoils from asserting that work should be a firm obligation.

Field recognises that not everyone will qualify for national insurance and urges the Benefits Agency to become 'pro-active'. Paying income support while awaiting return to work is no longer appropriate, he says.[27] All able-bodied people should be expected to plan their future, and he urges a start with the under-26 group, for whom income support should become a training allowance. Home visits are to be restored to discourage fraud, along with other deterrent measures—including daily signing-on at variable times.

In *Beyond Punishment* he and Matthew Owen also argue for Restart interviews and 'short-term training' to be compulsory, but they argue strongly against compulsory training and work in most cases. They explicitly reject the approach taken by Lawrence Mead in his earlier book, *Beyond Entitlement*, elaborated and defended in *The New Politics of Poverty*.

Mead's conclusion in *The New Politics of Poverty* is that participation in work should be required because, unless it is compulsory, schemes do not reach the hardest cases. They tend only to find work for people who would have gone back anyway.

Organisers of the Massachusetts workfare scheme have argued that if clients are compelled to work, they will not be well motivated.[28] However, in Massachusetts only about one-third of those eligible participated because the tendency was for clients not to turn up or to give in very easily. To overcome this problem, Mead found that administrators of workfare schemes in New York, Michigan, Oregon and Texas favoured compulsion.[29] In San Diego, for example, once they had joined the job search workshops, fewer than 10 per cent dropped out except to take a job.[30] The key to overcoming defeatism was not so much punishment, but case management. Two-thirds of staff time was devoted to chasing 'no shows', and clients did not resist but came to see the chasing as a sign of concern. Surveys of clients in Maryland, San Diego, Chicago, Arkansas and West Virginia found that they welcomed workfare and believed it had done them some good.[31] It was not that they were forced to accept outside values, as some critics claimed, but that they were required to act according to their own values. Authority, says Mead, 'operates as the midwife, not the antithesis, of freedom'.[32]

'Incentives' have been tried repeatedly. For instance, measures introduced in 1962 and 1967 allowed recipients of AFDC to keep about one-third of their earnings plus work expenses. There was no discernible influence on work effort. When Reagan removed most of these incentives in 1981, it also appeared to make no difference to work effort.[33] Mead's conclusion is that the problem is *not* that social reform is necessary to remove 'barriers' or 'traps', but that those dependent on benefits should come under gentle but firm pressure to find a job, for their own good. As he puts it:

> 'Making work pay' is popular because it suggests that the poor respond to the same suasions as the middle class. But the people who respond to incentives are mainly those who are already functional... No incentive has shown a power to pull many people across the line from non-work to work. For that, stronger medicine is required. *Incentives assume competence; the need is to create it.*[34]

Field's rejection of Mead's view highlights one of the main obstacles to rational discussion of public policy. There is a tendency to give blind allegiance to a faction or party and automatically to oppose the arguments of rival factions or parties. Field, as a Labour MP, is on 'the left' and so he must oppose 'the right', even if he agrees with them on particular points. Thus, in *Beyond Punishment* he argues that:

> The Right has cleverly argued its case largely in terms of what is best for the claimant. Long-term unemployment, they contend, leads to a demoralisation of individuals who need to be re-motivated back into work.[35]

By 'clever' he really means that there is truth in what they say, but because of his reluctance to agree with people who are supposed to be his opponents he attributes malign motives to them. He is:

> deeply suspicious of the Right's campaign, which often amounts to little more than thinking up new wheezes by which to bash the poor so as to reduce the public deficit.[36]

A fundamental requirement for rational debate is that participants do not falsely attribute ulterior motives to opponents. Field could have pointed out the differences between his view and Mead's without accusing him of secretly desiring to 'bash the poor'.

The Alternative

If the above criticisms of Field's approach are valid, what might an alternative and more workable reform look like? Now is not the time to suggest a lengthy alternative programme, but the guiding principles of such a scheme have already been set out in my book *Community Without Politics*.[37] What follows is a summary.

Field wants to reduce the qualifying time for national insurance to 13 weeks work to eliminate the disincentives produced by means testing. Income support does discourage the second partner from taking work, and it does make part-time work less attractive. Field is correct to claim that a national insurance benefit would formally remove these disincentives, but the recipient of a national insurance benefit would have no more of an incentive to take a full-time job than under income support, and might well face a reduced incentive, depending on the size of the benefit and the duration of payment.

The underlying difficulty is that if benefits are payable only to those who meet certain conditions, then some people will manage their affairs to qualify. Field assumes that it is only means testing that has this effect, but in practice it applies to all qualifying conditions, whether behavioural or financial.

Efforts to devise systems that are humane without producing unwanted behavioural change have encountered two main problems. First, because individual circumstances vary so much, it is impossible to devise rules that give the right material incentive or send the most desirable moral messages in all cases. Any rule is bound to be too severe in some cases and too lax in others. Consequently, it is desirable to vary any help given according to each individual's predicament. Second, reform cannot rely on material incentives alone. We should not fall into the trap of talking abstractly about the poor. Every person has his or her own story and each should receive personal attention in the hope of early restoration to independence. As longitudinal studies show, some people escape from poverty and some do not.[38] We should try to understand what enabled some to extricate themselves from poverty and ask whether the lessons can be taught to others.

Above all, public policies should appeal to the strengths of those being helped and not their weaknesses. By its nature, there is a danger that any benefit system—whatever the intentions of its designers—will be seen as a reward for irresponsibility and an inducement to avoid work. Replacement of means testing by an unconditional entitlement to benefit does not automatically overcome this danger.

An alternative scheme can be summarised as follows. First, anyone who has been unemployed for longer than six months should be the subject of intensive efforts, preferably by voluntary organisations, but if not by officials, to discover why they are not coping with the circumstances they find themselves in. If there is something that can be done to help, then it should be done. It may be that they are demoralised, in which case confidence-building is required; it may be a lack of workplace or social skills, in which case training may be called for; or they may have a bad employment record, so the challenge is to find an employer who will give them a second, third or fourth chance. The regime should never be purely punitive but also go hand in hand with offers of help, repeated daily. The intention is that benefits for the able bodied should be paid only in return for work or suitable training.

Second, earnings disregards and capital allowances should be abolished for all able-bodied and non-elderly recipients of income support, whilst simultaneously allowing claimants to opt to receive support from a voluntary organisation instead of the Benefits Agency. Voluntary organisations should be free to disregard earnings or savings as they believe best in each separate case. As experience of workfare shows, an administrative agency can accomplish a good deal, but it is more likely that voluntary organisations will achieve the right balance between mutual respect and the pressure that is required to restore individuals to independence. Historically, voluntary organisations were committed to the view that everyone had good in them and that their main task was to bring it out. It is not a matter of pointing a finger of blame, but of mounting an exhaustive search for the best in people, so that they can become free contributors to the good of all. I fully understand the reluctance to embrace compulsion, but as American workfare schemes show, the beneficiaries welcome it as symbolic of the genuine concern for their well-being that it truly represents. To restore to the workplace someone who has become demoralised or developed self-destructive attitudes is to encourage them to lead a fuller and better life.

Third, restoration of a role for voluntary organisations would have a further value. Not only will they be more likely to do a better, more intensive, job for the unemployed, there is also much to be gained from the reconstruction of civil society. For it was non-government organisations that upheld the ethos of self-improvement and service which has fallen into disrepair. (A fuller justification of this claim can be found in *Community Without Politics*.) Thus, a good deal could be accomplished by administrative reform, but a great deal more could be achieved by focusing also on the restoration of civil society. We have allowed ourselves to forget the importance of strong intermediate associations in maintaining what Field calls 'the verities of civilised life' (above, p. 9).

Pensions and Choice

Pension reform raises very different issues from the problem of welfare dependency already discussed, not least because some of the recipients of state benefits are not at present making a success of their lives and the challenge is to find ways of restoring (or creating) the missing capacity for self-management, whether through morale building or the provision of social and workplace skills. Pension reform is about ending unjustified public-sector monopoly.

Most Western countries have a state pension of some kind, whether funded on a pay-as-you-go basis or by earmarked taxes (national insurance or social security contributions). Three alternatives are generally put forward. The first requires payment of compulsory contributions but allows individuals a choice of pension provider. It is defended by proponents like Field as increasing choice compared with a scheme requiring a compulsory contribution to a state pension.

The second approach urges free market provision but calls for the government to encourage locked-in savings by means of tax breaks. The main line of reasoning used in support of this method is that people are short-sighted and, without encouragement, will not choose the most suitable means of saving, which is said to be the pension (or deferred annuity).

The third approach, and the one I will defend, prefers to put few, if any, limits on the methods by which people can provide for their old age and also opposes the use of the tax system to encourage particular types of provision. The government in this view should neither discriminate between methods of provision, nor require contributions to any given scheme. But, it has a responsibility to provide an income safety net for those who fail to provide for themselves for whatever reason.

Field calls for every person, employed or self-employed, to be compelled to contribute to a private pension.[39] He goes a little further than most socialists by advocating personal choice of pension provider. But why require a compulsory contribution at all?

First, in a free society people should accept responsibility for their own upkeep and that of their children throughout life. Since we know that death is certain and a period of old age likely, we have a duty to make provision for self-support until death, unless we are incapable of doing so. Second, we should assume competence for self-management, contrary to the dominant assumption of the twentieth century that most people need to have their affairs supervised by the authorities.

The duty of self-support means that we should only retire when we can afford it. If we have not saved enough to buy an annuity of sufficient size then we cannot afford to retire, and we need to carry on working until we can. The very idea of retiring from work is quite recent. Well into the twentieth century it was common for people to carry on working as long as possible. Friendly society members, for example, did so with the fall-back of sick pay, which they found it necessary to claim with greater frequency as they grew older. Perhaps we should think of ending work more gradually than has become the custom, and for savings to be adapted accordingly. Locking savings into a deferred annuity scheme, which requires the purchase of an annuity on a given retirement date, is too inflexible.

The only good argument for compulsion is that, because the state will not let anyone starve, the taxpayer can justly expect all individuals to contribute during their working life to a pension sufficient to meet the state minimum. The case for a compulsory scheme sufficient to provide a safety-net pension is based on a sense of reciprocal duty, but to require provision beyond the minimum, rests on the assumption that people are not competent and in need of paternalistic supervision.

One way of ensuring that everyone who can contribute does so, would be for the state to establish a defined contribution scheme that would require sufficient payments to produce a target capital value calculated to allow an annuity to be purchased that is equivalent to the safety net amount. Once this minimum level of saving had been reached, further saving would be optional. Individuals would be free to transfer their basic pension between providers. On retirement they would have to buy the minimum annuity required by law (the safety net amount). Any balance over that necessary to buy the minimum annuity could be taken as a lump sum, used to buy an additional annuity, or left to accumulate further interest.[40] The age at which the benefit system ceases to expect work should be raised to 70, in stages. People remain fit for much longer than in the past and this increasing longevity should be reflected in the benefit system.

After fulfilling this obligation to accumulate a pension fund sufficient to buy an annuity equivalent to the state minimum, individuals ought to be free to save as they wish. They could tie their money up in a deferred annuity or save it in such a way as to allow earlier access, or they could combine saving with insurance against contingencies like ill health. This would allow individuals to make provision for all their lifecycle needs, thus achieving independence. People may wish to save in preparation for predictable lifecycle changes, such as old age and having children; to protect against contingencies like illness; to acquire assets; to invest in a business; or to leave a sum of money to children. There are also many who will be capable of self-support only through mutual insurance, as the history of the friendly societies shows.

We all face different circumstances and we should be free to make suitable arrangements. This is especially true for the self-employed or those with small businesses. It may be to their advantage to build up their business rather than to pay into a pension; or to purchase property for later sale or to yield an income; or to purchase shares.

In addition, the nature of work has altered. Earlier in the century, it was possible to assume that most people were employees, but this is no longer true. The labour market continues to change, with fewer workers now expecting to spend their career with one employer and more working part-time. By 1994 17 per cent of men in work were self-employed, up from 10 per cent in 1975.[41] For all these reasons, the more flexibility the better, to allow variations in saving patterns, gaps, sudden bursts of effort, or a change of strategy from reliance on dividends or interest to capital growth. In a fast-changing world people should not have one hand tied behind their back by a well-meaning, but misguided, paternalistic state.

The same criticisms can be directed against tax incentives. This approach does not employ direct compulsion, but it is also based on mistrust of personal choice. Tax breaks are designed to make long-term lock-in of savings more attractive. But there is no reason to suppose that such inducement is wise, not least because tax inducements not only reduce the individual's ability to make appropriate arrangements for his unique circumstances, but also diminish competition to the extent that companies can attract funds for reasons other than their investment performance.

Tax incentives may lead to schemes which impose heavy charges on consumers in ways which are not fully transparent. And such schemes allow all or part of the tax concession to be creamed off in charges or commissions to brokers. No less important, tax concessions lead to regulation, since any government must stipulate the type of pension that qualifies. Such regulations diminish the ability of the financial services industry to respond to the wide variety of personal requirements.

To summarise: under a voluntary framework, the state would continue to maintain a safety net, it would regulate in the interests of competition and choice, and provide useful comparative information to strengthen the hand of the consumer and to enhance competition. Social solidarity would no longer be based on the dubious claim that pensioners have a claim to share in current wages, but instead on the far stronger bond of knowing that each takes personal responsibility for his or her own upkeep in order not to be a burden on others, and on the knowledge that no one—either through misfortune or bad judgement—will be allowed to fall below a certain point.

Table 1
Work Effort of Households,
Before Deduction of Housing Costs, 1961-1991

	1961	1976	1991
Bottom Quintile			
- self-employed	8.18	8.81	9.37
- single or couple, all in full-time work	5.73	2.89	1.54
- one full-time, one part-time	5.84	2.52	1.73
- one full-time, one not working	24.95	18.16	7.90
- one or more in part-time work	5.60	6.09	7.16
- head or spouse 60 or over	32.27	36.21	29.47
- head or spouse unemployed	2.34	12.40	20.06
- other	15.09	12.93	21.97
	100%	100%	100%
Total population			
- self-employed	7.38	6.72	9.88
- single or couple, all in full-time work	23.46	24.43	23.46
- one full-time, one part-time	13.44	17.30	13.76
- one full-time, one not working	36.29	24.48	14.62
- one or more in part-time work	2.59	4.95	6.18
- head or spouse 60 or over	11.60	14.03	17.62
- head or spouse unemployed	0.68	3.48	5.97
- other	4.58	4.61	8.52
	100%	100%	100%
Top Decile			
- self-employed	14.04	13.59	14.16
- single or couple, all in full-time work	46.94	53.96	46.45
- one full-time, one part-time	7.18	11.32	10.43
- one full-time, one not working	22.85	13.70	15.13
- one or more in part-time work	1.01	2.69	3.51
- head or spouse 60 or over	6.07	2.78	7.67
- head or spouse unemployed	0.00	0.40	0.50
- other	1.91	1.55	2.16
	100%	100%	100%

Source: Alissa Goodman and Steven Webb, *For Richer, For Poorer: the Changing Distribution of Income in the United Kingdom, 1961-91,* London: Institute for Fiscal Studies, 1994, pp. 27-28, A15, A28, A29.

Table 2
Households and Economic Activity, 1994/95

Number of economically active persons in household	Decile Group									
	Lowest	2	3	4	5	6	7	8	9	Highest
None	76.9	78.1	66.7	44.4	29.6	14.5	9.1	6.1	4.1	2.2
One person	20.9	19.7	26.4	43.2	45.3	40.1	32.0	25.1	17.3	18.1
Two persons	2.0	2.2	6.3	10.9	22.7	40.6	48.9	55.3	56.1	53.6
Three persons	0.0	0.0	0.6	1.5	1.7	3.9	9.9	10.9	18.7	16.6
Four or more	0.1	0.0	0.0	0.0	0.6	0.9	1.2	2.5	3.8	9.5
	100%	100%	100%	100%	100%	100%	100%	100%	100%	100%

Source: *Family Spending: A Report on the 1994/95 Family Expenditure Survey*, London: HMSO, 1995, Table 9.7.

Notes

1 Field, F., *Making Welfare Work: Reconstructing Welfare for the Millennium*, London: Institute of Community Studies, 1995, p. 2.

2 *Making Welfare Work*, p. 124.

3 In Brittan, S., *Left or Right: The Bogus Dilemma*, London: Secker and Warburg, 1968; and Brittan, S., *Capitalism and the Permissive Society*; London: Macmillan, 1973.

4 *Making Welfare Work, op. cit.*, p. 148.

5 *Making Welfare Work*, p. 150.

6 Employment Committee, *The Right to Work/Workfare*, Minutes of Evidence, Session 1994-95, 31-i, p. 21.

7 Each partner can earn £5 without deduction of income support.

8 *Making Welfare Work*, pp. 32-34.

9 Tax/Benefit Model Tables, April 1995, p. 3.3.

10 Mead, L., *The New Politics of Poverty*, New York: Basic Books, 1992, p. 7.

11 *The New Politics of Poverty*, p. 7.

12 *Ibid.*, p. 9.

13 *Ibid.*, p. 89.

14 *Ibid.*, p. 171.

15 Harkness, S., Machin, S. and Waldfogel, J., *Evaluating the Pin Money Hypothesis: The Relationship Between Women's Labour Market Activity, Family Income and Poverty in Britain*, London School of Economics Welfare State Programme, May 1995, p. 7.

16 Harkness *et al.*, p. 8.

17 Harkness *et al.*, p. 10.

18 Harkness *et al.*, pp. 19-22.

19 Harkness *et al.*, pp. 21-22.

20 Harkness *et al.*, p. 28.

21 Spiegelman, R. and Yaeger, K., 'The Seattle and Denver Income Maintenance Experiments: Overview', *The Journal of Human Resources*, Vol. XV, No. 4, Fall 1980, p. 468.

22 Groeneveld, L., Tuma, N., and Hannan, M., 'The Effects of Negative Income Tax on Marital Dissolution', *The Journal of Human Resources*, Vol. XV, No. 4, Fall 1980, pp. 654-74.

23 Robins, P., Tuma, N. and Yaeger, K., 'Effects of SIME/DIME on Changes in Employment Status', *The Journal of Human Resources*, Vol. XV, No. 4, Fall 1980, p. 566.

24 West, R., 'Effects on the Labour Supply of Young Nonheads', *The Journal of Human Resources*, Vol. XV, No. 4, Fall 1980, p. 587.

25 To put the question in this way does not imply that morals and material incentives are incompatible. Cash benefits have a moral signalling effect as well as a mere incentive effect; and a morally good person could respond unselfishly to material rewards.

26 For a fuller discussion see Green, D.G., *Reinventing Civil Society*, London: IEA Health and Welfare Unit, 1993.

27 *Making Welfare Work*, p. 32.

28 *The New Politics of Poverty*, p. 172.

29 *The New Politics of Poverty*, p. 173.

30 *The New Politics of Poverty*, p. 174.

31 *The New Politics of Poverty*, pp. 173-74.

32 *The New Politics of Poverty*, p. 172.

33 *The New Politics of Poverty*, p. 161.

34 *The New Politics of Poverty*, p. 162; emphasis added.

35 Field, F., and Owen, M., *Beyond Punishment: Hard Choices on the Road to Full Employability*, London: Institute of Community Studies, 1994, p. 2.

36 *Beyond Punishment*, p. 78.

37 London: IEA, 1996.

38 Bane, M.J. and Ellwood, D.T., 'Slipping into and out of Poverty: The Dynamics of Spells', *Journal of Human Resources*, Vol. 21, 1986, pp. 1-23; Buck, N., Gershuny, J., Rose, D. and Scott, J., *Changing Households: the British Household Panel Survey, 1990-1992*, Colchester: ESRC Research Centre on Micro-social Change, 1994.

39 *Making Welfare Work*, p. 177.

40 A scheme with some of these features has been advocated by Sir Roger
    Douglas, in *Unfinished Business,* Auckland: Random House, 1993, pp.
    164-65.

41 General Household Survey, 1994, London: HMSO, p. 206.

Welfare and the Common Good

Melanie Phillips

THE Labour Party's claim to be the party of social conscience is defined above all by its attitude towards the welfare state. Of all the issues—and there are many—which give rise to general alarm that the party has lost its soul, the relief of poverty is perhaps the most sensitive of all. If the party's supporters collectively conclude that it has given up on the poor, then they might as well all pack their bags and go home. The issue of poverty acts as the litmus test of Labour's moral sense. It tells us whether the party remains committed above all to promoting the welfare of others and the maintenance of a social ethic, or whether it is now entirely devoted to the pursuit of selfish individualism.

Merely putting it like that, however, immediately begs a few questions. Labour has told itself a story in which it occupies the moral high ground where it lays sole claim to virtues such as compassion and altruism. It lays such a claim because of its historical roots in ethical socialism and before that in the precepts of the Evangelical and Methodist movements which furnished the moral base for the political principles of the emerging Labour Party. But this noble inheritance has blinded it to the ways in which subsequent thinking was allowed to corrupt those early principles. In place of its founding commitment to the welfare of others, in came militant individualism in which the predominant ethic was no longer duty but individual rights. In place of a clear sense of right and wrong behaviour defined as such by its effects on others, in came non-judgmentalism which is inimical to a moral sense. In place of individual responsibility came a Marxist world-view which represented individuals as the helpless tools of economic circumstances beyond their control and in which materialism became the dominant value. And in place of the meritocracy to which the early ethical socialists were committed, instead of the equality of opportunity which would enable individuals to better themselves, in came egalitarianism which, in direct contrast, sought to equalise not opportunity but achievement.

The impact of these altered attitudes upon welfare has been hard to overestimate. The confusion of poverty with inequality meant that, instead of drawing poor people into the national project to create wealth, they were to become merely the passive recipients of wealth that had already been created and had to be taken off someone else. Since no moral judgments could be entered, considerations of character and behaviour—which had been axiomatic to early welfare pioneers such as

Beveridge or Tawney—became taboo. People could therefore behave as badly as they liked confident in the knowledge that the state would pay out benefits regardless. That was everyone's 'right'. 'Blaming the poor' became synonymous with 'blaming the victim'. In the general victim culture that had developed, the poor were the ultimate victims and therefore all judgment of their actions was to be suspended. Drawing attention to benefit fraud, say, was considered to be the ultimate in bad form, far worse than the fraud itself. Similarly, questioning the wisdom of benefit dependency was considered a further assault on disadvantaged people—even though dependency could hardly have been thought to be to their advantage.

The outcome was a set of conundrums. High moral principles had created a welfare culture in which dishonesty and fraud had become routine. Well-meaning 'liberals' had deprived poor people of the self-respect due to autonomous moral agents. Intent above all on making themselves feel good about their benevolence towards the poor, these high minded paternalists used the jargon of 'empowerment' but actually kept a tight grip on the incomes of the poor. Instead of enabling them to better themselves, they deprived them of the means to escape their poverty by drawing up networks of rules to discourage them from working. The misguided attempt to separate economic from moral and personal characteristics created a dilemma. The welfare state had replaced a piecemeal system which had failed to meet society's needs. But in doing so, it had destroyed the voluntary networks that sustained the concept of community, thus undermining those civic values on which society depended. The result was that the value-free policies designed to avoid stigma and shame betrayed the very people they were ostensibly designed to protect.

A Return to Character

Frank Field is the one politician on the left who has broken the taboo on discussing these dilemmas and paradoxes. His great achievement is not merely to open up this debate but to attempt to re-site welfare within its original framework of moral judgments. Unlike other suggestions for reform, his proposals are grounded in a coherent philosophy. He has understood that a strategy that simply attempts to relieve poverty, which is defined as not having as much as other people, will inevitably trap people in that poverty rather than free them from it. He has recognised that, as often as not, poor people are not passive victims but potentially active agents in their own regeneration. And he is forcing us to ask the great questions about our civic organisation. Do we still want the state to provide for us? How much are we prepared to pay to meet the needs of others? Will the better-off ever again be willing to redistribute money to pay for the poor? Where should the line be drawn between the state's duty towards its citizens and the duty of citizens towards themselves and each other?

A return to considerations of character does not necessarily deny the impact of factors beyond the control of individuals. Macro-economic policies, unemployment and the failures in the education system clearly play key roles in the creation of poverty; not to mention a population ever more top-heavy with ageing and increasingly frail dependents. But different individuals react differently to similar circumstances. It is surely as wrong to deny the impact of people's attitudes and behaviour on their situation as it would be to deny the impact of developments such as widespread factory closures.

Field is correct to point out that the current welfare system exacerbates such problems rather than solves them. Social security has turned into a culture of social insecurity, and not just because of the significant redistribution of income from the poor to the rich that has taken place since 1979. In one of the many paradoxes of Thatcherism, the doctrine of the minimum state gave rise to maximum dependency through the huge rise in unemployment that took place. In addition, longer lives and family disintegration have put pressures on Beveridge's welfare state which it was never designed to withstand. But Field's point is that the mammoth welfare bill very often throws good money after bad. The more that is spent, the more people are caught in the poverty traps that have resulted from the massive rise in means-tested benefits. Under the impact of such daunting external pressures, the welfare system hinders rather than helps individual efforts to overcome them. As he says, it penalises thrift, honesty and work and encourages instead dishonesty, opportunism and idleness.

Poverty

Field's proposals provide an opportunity to end the sterile argument about definitions which undermines the clear thinking needed to tackle poverty. The right recognise only absolute poverty, defined as an absence of the fundamentals of human existence such as clean drinking water, food or shelter. The left favour a definition of relative poverty, measured by the number of material goods enjoyed by most people at a given time which are denied to a section of the community which cannot afford them. Neither of these definitions, however, is very helpful. The absolutists merely state the obvious when they say that people drawing their welfare giros enjoy material benefits they wouldn't have had 50 years ago. So what? Just because the outside privy is now largely a thing of the past hardly means that no household with an indoor lavatory can be poor. The relativists, on the other hand, claim that poverty is defined as a level of income below half the average. But since average incomes have risen, taking upwards those below the average to a higher standard of living, at what point do those people stop being poor? It is an argument over whether the level of benefit is sufficient—but sufficient for what? On this, there can be no agreement. Yet these are the flaky assumptions which have governed welfare policy for several decades.

Any attempt to deal with poverty on this basis by redistributing income will fail. The absence of any consensus about what poverty is guarantees resentment among the better off. As Field observes, altruism through general redistribution is no longer a tenable proposition. Anti-poverty programmes not only patronise and disempower poor people but also alienate the better-off. The state can and must provide the opportunities, but ultimately the only people who can combat poverty are the poor themselves. Yet here as elsewhere, while the analysis is brave and true, the practical remedy is problematic. For example, Field does not rule out redistribution altogether. His proposed insurance corporation would pay benefits to unemployed and low paid people from the contributions of the better-off. He believes that such targeted and above-board redistribution would command general understanding and agreement which at present is lacking.

It is tempting to share his optimism that such a hypothecation would prompt a moribund public generosity back into life. But it's very much a moot point, particularly given the scale of the subsidy the better-off would be required to make. It is also unclear how this subsidy fits with Field's anti-dependency, pro-active income support agency which would make work or training a condition of benefit. He argues with passion for inclusiveness, intrinsic to his stakeholder concept, which means that the very poor must not be left out of the proposed new welfare settlement. Inclusiveness is a fine ideal; but since the whole idea is to break the cycle of dependency by making the connection explicit between what people pay in and what they get out, such a subvention by the better-off appears to be a contradiction. Moreover, it is not at all clear that the better-off would cheerfully shell out for every category of poor person. Implicit in Field's proposals is the probability that some categories of people (young able-bodied men? single parents?) might not command sufficient public sympathy to merit such a subsidy. We'd be back to the distinction between the deserving and the undeserving poor.

Such a distinction is anathema to so-called liberals. It is precisely the abhorrence of making it that has led to the value-neutral welfare system which connives at dishonesty and so horrifies Field. These welfare 'liberals' see the poor wholly as victims of circumstances. The idea that some of them might, through a change in their behaviour, haul themselves out of poverty, the black market and petty crime offends such commentators as badly as welfare cheating offends Field. But the value-neutral welfare system we have now means that the taxpayer is subsidising, to some extent at least, behaviour that is antisocial and undesirable. That seems to be as self-destructive a form of social organisation as it is unjust.

Certainly, the situation of the poor at present is wretched. Given the current structure of welfare, the cheese-paring savings made to the system have been mean-spirited and harsh, making a bad situation even more difficult. Worse still, as Field observes, the cuts made in national insurance benefits have been nothing less than a swindle. But one only has to look at different groups of poor people to recognise that cultural factors are indissolubly linked to material circumstances. Poverty is not merely an absence of material benefits. It is also a spiritual, emotional, moral and cultural state. It embraces inadequacy on many different fronts simultaneously. In the houses of the very poor, expensive children's bikes, trainers and video games often testify either to catastrophic money mismanagement or to a thriving black economy, drug culture and crime. In a frightening number of poor families, material deprivation appears to have been upstaged by the new evils of an alternative moral universe.

Yet this is by no means universal. There are many households which retain their moral integrity despite their poverty. It is noticeable how people from the Asian subcontinent, for example, who settle in Britain and who may be very poor, who may live in wholly unsuitable accommodation and be inadequately educated, nevertheless seem to possess the initiative to attempt to struggle out of poverty, or at least to push their children out of it. Of course, one might legitimately point out that these are very different cultures in which family structure, in particular, is notably intact; there may be poverty but there tends not to be the accompanying emotional and spiritual chaos which trap so many very poor families in their vicious cycle. But that's just the point. There's nothing inevitable about persistent disadvantage. People react very differently to the same adversities. Poverty is a cultural construct. And more creative and energetic cultural responses can be learnt.

Altruism and Self-interest

Field's proposals seek to return welfare to the original assumption made by Beveridge, Tawney and Temple that welfare and character are indissolubly linked. We do have a moral duty to help those who really can't help themselves, but we've redefined the notion of helplessness far too broadly. Welfare and character work upon each other. Once, it was vitally important to thinkers on the left to recognise the unalterable moral responsibility of every individual regardless of circumstances. To think otherwise was to demean their humanity. That perception has been lost. Welfare must involve not just the discharge of the duty of the state towards individuals but the duty of individuals towards themselves and others. Field offers the foundation for a new, third way in politics: not statism which 'does unto' people; nor the minimum state, market model in which individuals are left to fend for themselves while the weak go to the wall; but a community based on reciprocal duties and shared effort, prudence and mutual responsibility. He offers an alternative to the current Hobson's choice: between, on the one hand, those who see poverty as the outcome of economic determinism and capitalist malevolence, and on the other those who see the poor merely as specimens of flawed human nature.

He also understands that any system has to go with the grain of human nature if it is to work. That means acknowledging the primacy of self-interest. Altruism plays a role in this vision, but it is secondary and carefully defined as the handmaiden of that self-interest. This is easily caricatured as a pale imitation of Thatcherism. But that is surely to miss the point. This is a different idea of self from the Thatcherite model, in which the self stands in opposition to society. Selfishness and greed have no place, however, in Field's universe. It is rather a return to the Victorian idea of self. As Gertrude Himmelfarb wrote, to the Victorians 'the individual, or self, was the ally rather than the adversary of society'.[1] To the Victorians, 'self' meant helping one's neighbour, a sense of duty to others, an awareness of the needs of other people that is so lacking today. It meant self-discipline and self-control for the benefit of others.

Self-interest as thus defined makes us all part of a larger whole and relates our individual actions to the general good. Field defines it explicitly not as selfishness but as a set of opposite virtues such as hard work and honesty. The interest thus defined is in realising the higher aspirations of the self, or moral character. He realises that if these characteristics are thwarted, it is our humanity itself which will atrophy. This is a concept of the self that has largely disappeared from public discourse during the Conservative years. It is also a fundamentally religious perspective which has all but vanished from mainstream pulpits.

It follows from this that he reintroduces the concept of conditionality into welfare, which means that welfare must act to encourage and reward good behaviour and enhance those roles which the country values, while discouraging and failing to reward behaviour which is damaging or antisocial. This proposal, however, rests upon an assumption which is deeply contested by 'liberals': the notion of a common good. Actions can only be regarded as operating against the public interest if there is a clearly defined and universally accepted public interest to be defended. But our culture of atomised individualism recognises as valid only freedom, rights and choice. To a society which worships at the shrine of subjectivity, the common good is an anathema. The custodians of our social policy, our cultural élites who often appear to inhabit a different moral universe from the majority of people, consider that the common good is by definition authoritarian. Setting out a set of explicit values for society is considered oppressive because it seeks to impose one view upon everyone. Since this corrupted liberalism means that everyone's view is considered of equal value to everyone else's, that all judgment is pro-scribed and all hierarchies of value are taboo, the common good is dismissed as illiberal. Yet without it there can be no civic culture or civic morality. Pro-social behaviour embodies virtues such as responsibility, thrift, hard work, prudence. The state has a legitimate interest in promoting such virtues because otherwise it cannot help engender a civic ethic of mutual responsibility and co-operation.

Marriage and Lone Parenthood

A prime example of the common good at work is the institution of marriage. Marriage is a bridge between private behaviour and civic order. It is a contract whose purpose is to hold a couple together by the most formal and binding method a society can devise in order to ensure that their children are adequately socialised and that rights to property are protected. If these aspects are not safeguarded, disorder follows. Since such disorder is against the public interest, the state has an interest in preventing it. The state should therefore promote marriage as a common good through law and through the tax and benefits system. But at present it does not do so. This is not the place to discuss the flaws in the 1996 Family Law Bill, but, as Patricia Morgan has demonstrated in *Farewell to the Family*[2] and other works, taxes and benefits currently discriminate against married couples and in favour of lone mothers. This is a perverse incentive that needs to be corrected because lone parenthood, generally speaking, is not an ideal state in which to raise children. The state can't afford to claim neutrality between married and unmarried motherhood while in effect subsidising the conditions for progressive social dislocation.

Field, however, does not address this point as such. Instead, he suggests a structural change in the approach to single parents, under which they would be offered education or training as a condition of benefit in order to get them out to work. This, however, surely indicates a significant flaw in his thinking. He has placed too much emphasis on the role of welfare and too little on a range of massive cultural forces in his attempt to contain family breakdown and the rise and rise of the young, never-married mother.

As he says, single parenthood is a major cause of family poverty and one which far outstrips unemployment. And it is certainly true that this cause of poverty tends to be minimised by people determined to blame it all on the state. However, the relationship between family structure and poverty is highly complicated. As Patricia Morgan has shown, there is now a far greater extent of poverty among single-earner, two-parent families than among lone parents. This is because of the combination of low pay with a tax and benefits system which favours lone parents. Child poverty, in other words, is caused by other factors than family fragmentation or unemployment.

And other factors than welfare have also intersected to promote lone parenthood. Unemployment and low pay have between them brought about a dearth of young men who can earn enough to become a marriageable proposition. There is also a complex of powerful cultural factors: the collapse of any stigma attached to children born out of wedlock, for example; or the way in which the cultural primacy of the woman's 'right' to either conceive or get rid of an unborn child, courtesy of medical technology, has reduced children to mere extensions of the mother's ego; or the way in which abortion and contraception have altered the dynamics of the relationship between men and women; or the network of soaring aspirations, inability to weather conflict and collapse of the notion of commitment that has contributed to the rising number of divorces. In other words, Charles Murray is wrong. Welfare cannot be held responsible for the imploding family unit. It's much more complicated than that. Cutting lone mothers out of welfare won't stop families breaking up or young girls having babies. But what welfare should *not* do is what it now does do: encourage single motherhood by rewarding it and penalising marriage. In other words, welfare is currently helping make a bad situation worse. That can be remedied, however, by reversing those incentives so that the tax and benefit system favours marriage rather than un-marriage.

But Field is wrong to argue that the problem will be solved if lone parents are helped into the labour market. Indeed, his analysis here is flawed. As he observes, unemployment is nowhere near as large a cause of poverty as single motherhood. Yet his 'remedy' for the increase in single parents is to get lone mothers into the labour market. He implies, therefore, that the single mother's main problem is that she is poor, and that her poverty results from the fact that she hasn't got a job. But this isn't so. The main problem with lone motherhood is not poverty but the fact that it is an undesirable state in which to bring up children. Working is an antidote to unemployment; but motherhood is not unemployment. Working will not solve the problems experienced by very young, never-married mothers; indeed, it may make them worse. Working motherhood is a complex juggling act that requires stamina, fortitude, single minded-ness, emotional strength and organisational skills: the very attributes that very young, never-married mothers conspicuously lack. It is not just the material poverty of their situation that disadvantages both themselves and their children; it is the emotional and practical chaos of their lives, and the impact on the children both of mothers who can't cope and the absence of their fathers.

Nor is work necessarily the solution to the problems of the more mature lone parent either. After all, one of the reasons why so many married men in full-time work are now poor is because their single wage is not enough to keep a family. Moreover, lone mothers at work would be even worse off because they would need to pay for childcare. And if that bill were picked up by the state, then society would once again be in the invidious position of subsidising an undesirable childrearing environment. The most likely result of a mass movement of lone mothers into the labour market would be their rise from destitution to poverty, with a corresponding increase in child neglect. And in addition, flooding the labour market with lone mothers would also deprive even more young men of work, thus exacerbat-ing the phenomenon of the unmarriageable male which contributed to the increase in lone parents in the first place.

In short, welfare hasn't caused the disintegration of the family and ending welfare for lone parents will not address that phenomenon.

Welfare certainly should not continue, however, to favour or subsidise lone parenthood but should provide incentives for marriage instead. Family breakdown, if it can be slowed down at all, needs to be tackled by a comprehensive programme of public education, law and welfare support systems. In his commendable anxiety to reintroduce character into the welfare debate, Field has gone too far in downplaying the part played by external cultural and economic factors in contributing to poverty. For example, important as it is that welfare should not contribute to work-shyness, there have to be jobs for people to go to. Unemployment cannot be licked simply through supply-side measures such as enhanced training. Macroeconomics also plays a critical role here. And the mantra of 'training' is currently worse than meaningless as a potential panacea because the quality of 'training' is abysmal. 'Training' will never create many jobs until politicians tackle its profound inadequacies, as well as the continuing disaster of an education system which throws so many young people on the scrapheap. Welfare and education are symbiotically linked. But simply providing more of the latter will not ease the pressure upon the former until both the structural and pedagogic failures of the education and training systems are put right.

Can It Work?

Field's central proposal, a national insurance corporation run jointly by members, employers and government representatives, is very attractive. It would restore not merely a sense of fairness but would introduce an explicit and transparent relationship between ourselves and the money held in trust on our behalf. The idea has grown up that state expenditure is somehow nothing to do with us. We are alienated from it even while we know it's ours. A proposal which restores a sense of ownership and attachment must be a good thing. Nevertheless, it may also be naïve. It is hard to imagine any government allowing such a huge and powerful body to exist independent of national government control.

Similarly, Field's idea of a private pension corporation is enticing. Mutual aid organisations, a form of collective endeavour outside the state, embody the communitarian philosophy of a third way that gives primacy neither to the state nor to the individual but creates instead a community of reciprocal support. But again, it must be doubtful whether people will trust the effective nationalisation of their private schemes. In theory, this may comprise social rather than state collectivism; but where's the guarantee of the dividing line to protect such an enterprise from the grasping hands of the Treasury and state control?

Field envisages that this welfare revolution would bring about a wholesale culture shift. He intends nothing less than the re-moralisation of Britain through the welfare system. The question, though, is whether any welfare system must be doomed to fail unless British society quite independently decides to change the fundamental assumptions on which it is currently founded. For example, Britain is not an opportunity or entrepreneurial culture. Too many people don't believe Britain has a future at all. The current education system could hardly be bettered as a means of keeping the poor poor. Subjectivity rules; authority and rules of behaviour have been eroded. The culture of rights promulgates irresponsibility and dishonesty and promotes a winner-take-all philosophy with no concern for the consequences for other people. How can Field's welfare system introduce judgment about character when judgment itself is taboo? How can welfare expect reciprocal duties from unemployed people or lone parents when working or bearing a child are regarded as rights rather than, as they should be, a set of duties? Can a welfare system really remoralise a society, or can we only achieve a virtuous welfare system if society becomes remoralised through other routes?

The answer is surely that the two must go together if either is to have any chance of succeeding. For all the specific caveats, the importance of Frank Field's proposals is that he opens the debate beyond welfare into that wider cutural arena where the balance between duties and rights needs to be significantly adjusted. Welfare doesn't create amoral or immoral behaviour but it does reinforce it. But if the current vicious cycle is to be transformed into a virtuous one, our establishment will have to abandon its damaging stance of value-neutrality and come out fighting for the common good.

Notes

1   Himmelfarb, G., *The Demoralization of Society,* London: IEA Health and Welfare Unit, 1995, p. 256.

2   Morgan, P., *Farewell to the Family*, London: IEA Health and Welfare Unit, 1995.

A Rejoinder

Frank Field

I AM grateful to each contributor for the attention and interest they have given to the ideas in *Making Welfare Work*. I should also like to thank the IEA Health and Welfare Unit for the publication and Alan Deacon for suggesting the idea and for seeing this project through to fruition. Politicians rarely enjoy the luxury of an opportunity to consider, in a non politically partisan manner, the criticisms of their peers. I am grateful to the IEA for allowing me the privilege to do so in the form of this paper. I shall attempt to deal in two ways with the main issues raised in these four essays. First I shall address the general questions or criticisms made about the framework of ideas within which I set the reconstruction of welfare. I shall then answer the individual criticisms.

Underlying many of Pete Alcock's criticisms is the belief that I have struck the wrong balance between self-interest and altruism. He is right to concentrate attention here for it is in this area that I am most anxious to see a fundamental reassessment of ideas by the centre-left in Britain. The Titmuss position which Alcock promotes is not tenable. Altruism alone is not a strong enough motivational force to sustain the sheer size of the welfare edifice as proposed by the Titmuss framework. Self-interest is the most powerful of our human dynamisms. To suggest otherwise is to ignore what is obvious to the human eye. Indeed, it is surely worth noting that altruism is most clearly expressed in the Titmuss scheme of things (it underpins of course his central belief that welfare should be given unconditionally) in the blood transfusion service. But membership here is voluntary and far from universal. Universalism is the objective which *Making Welfare Work* set out to achieve in welfare reconstruction and that objective cannot be met by the operation of the voluntary principle. Successful welfare reform entails much more than the running of a voluntary organisation.

I do not however advocate politics which enhance only self-interest. But not to take this as the starting point which influences the shape of what can then be proposed is more than merely folly. It is a recipe for disaster. My own proposal, rather, is to create policies which satisfy self-interest in a manner which is concomitant with the public good, i.e. that people gain what they want without simultaneously restraining their neighbour. That objective I have tried to pursue by the detailed policies which are developed in *How To Pay For The Future*.

There is another point at issue here. Any conversation with the electorate has to begin with a recognition of where the electorate is rather than any fantasy of where we might like to position them. Thatcherism has had a significant impact on the electorate's views. For over a decade a two-track war of attrition has been fought against the body of beliefs inculcated by the Coalition and Attlee Governments: negatively against the substantial legacy of 'my brother's keeper' of which British voters were still the heirs even twenty years ago, and positively by promoting unbridled self-interest which would have been termed by most 1945 voters as little less than unadulterated greed.

It is easier to destroy a tradition than it is to rebuild it. A mere plea for altruism, no matter how well intended, or eloquently articulated, will largely be rejected. An unspoken assumption of *Making Welfare Work* was that a new welfare settlement had to be made anyway. (The current arrangements are simply unsustainable, and are undesirable in some very important respects.) And the new arrangements should rightly appeal to self-interest. It was also implicit that once the schemes were shown to work and were strongly affirmed by voters as desirable, as well as effective, the altruistic element—perhaps better described as fellow-ship—which was inbuilt from the very beginning could be developed. Therefore, stage by stage, those outside the labour market would be brought into the new stakeholder welfare arrangement. Inclusion is by meeting their stakeholder payment, and not, as Alcock mistakenly believes, by merely making credits into their account. This distinction is far from trivial.

The plea for a rebuilding of a hardnosed altruistic spirit (i.e. people outside the labour market are awarded stakeholder status because their conduct is approved by the electorate) is based on the Christian ethic. The operative word here, of course, is 'based'. The Christian ideal is one of unconditional altruism. There is nothing conditional in the actions of the Good Samaritan, to cite but one familiar example. Ideals represent aspirations yet I do not believe that such selfless action is a realistic proposition for public as opposed to private conduct—another major difference between myself and the Titmuss ideal.

The distinction which is made between love (or altruism) and justice is crucial to my argument. Because love is by definition an unconditional motivational force it can, with few exceptions, only operate within a tightly knit group, and even here it is difficult enough to sustain. In contrast, justice may be a less perfect motivational force, for it is conditional and conditioned by a sense of fairness, but it has a universal application.

My Christian cosmology bears on the argument in another respect. One of Alan Deacon's criticisms is that my discussion of human nature is incomplete. In the context of the issues being discussed here I neither have the confidence to submit a thesis on human nature, nor do I consider such a detailed analysis relevant. What I seek to do is to build the foundations on to which a new welfare settlement is built which are true to human nature.

Words are all most of us have to express public and sometimes private feelings. But the more important the feelings or beliefs expressed the more limited words are in adequately conveying what is felt or believed. For me one of the great strengths and attractions of Christianity is how great truths are told in the form of simple stories. These stories, rooted, like those of Aesop, in a familiar generality of experience, allude to feelings and beliefs for which words alone can describe only the most superficial aspects.

For Christians the understanding of mankind begins with the Creation and the Fall, which two events are hardly separated in the text. But the story does not end, of course, with the Fall. We are less than perfect creatures and it is partly because of this most fundamental aspect of each of us that a distinction has continually to be made between where we are now and our destiny, on the one hand, and what might ideally be hoped for now in the bosom of the family and what can operate in the wider public arena, on the other.

My reflections on human nature therefore were simply to inform readers that I subscribed to a Christian understanding of mankind, and nothing which followed could be understood properly without an appreciation of this framework of belief. So my references to character (i.e. to our fallen nature) are highly relevant to the central position that I award to self-interest. Likewise, because of my belief in mankind's destiny to be redeemed, I assign to altruism the role of an ideal, which though not attainable in any full sense now, is what should be aimed for and which we are destined one day to achieve.

In expanding the framework of my beliefs I hope that I have suggested that many of the criticisms of detail which Alcock makes derive in part from his misunderstanding of how I view the political reform of welfare developing, the direction I believe it should take, and the values which both nurture the reforms and which will be nurtured themselves by its success. Similarly, I think he is also wrong in not setting welfare in the context of how an increasing global economy is impacting on the UK base, and how the shifting of the global advantage to the Pacific economies restrains rather than enhances the scope to reconstruct welfare here.

There are five other criticisms which Alcock makes and to which I would like to offer a rebuttal. First, he writes of my plea for 'a remoralisation of welfare'. That is a phrase I am not conscious of having used. Moralisation, for me, generates an image of a puritanical finger-wagging brigade to which I have no wish to be party. In Britain morals are too often seen as an endless list of negative instructions. The first story in the Bible is of God's creation which is seen as good and to be enjoyed. There were rules, of course, governing this enjoyment, but the instruction for enjoyment comes first. While I have written and spoken about rules embodying a clear sense of right and wrong, I have shied away from the use of morals. It would have been particularly foolish for a politician to offer moral instruction.

Two further criticisms can be taken together. In a world increasingly polarised along lines of income and race, Alcock views the plea for self-help as yet another force dividing society. He may be right, but not, I fear, in the way he sees the operation working. The move to the personal ownership of pension capital via mutual aid companies and friendly societies could see not only the Asian but West Indian British responding with enthusiasm. Ironically, the group that could be left behind here might well be the poorer whites.

Alcock likewise fails to accept the distinction I draw between state and collective provision. State-run welfare is on the decline. *Making Welfare Work* made a case for new forms of collective provision to which there are individual rights and ownership. Individual rights would be enshrined by the collective ownership of the scheme and the capital would be owned by its title deed.

A fourth disagreement centres on the extent and possibilities of redistribution. While Alcock sees redistribution in one dimensional terms, I view it as a fourfold possibility. *Making Welfare Work* proposes some redistribution between income groups. But it is more concerned with redistributing resources differently over a person's lifetime, within households, and above all between households in respect of access to the labour market. The most significant growth in inequality since 1979 has been in household income and this has primarily been brought about by the growth of the no-wage/two- or three- or more wage households. National insurance changes, together with the new employment benefit qualifying rules, are aimed at sharing out more fairly the new jobs which are created at any one time within the economy. Here is a most fundamental redistribution which has nothing to do with using the Exchequer to take money from workers to give to non-workers.

Lastly I think Alcock misunderstands the nature of the changes I propose. I no longer see a solution to poverty simply in terms of higher benefits. Indeed, the extension of coverage, and the rise in the value of means tests (taking only 22 per cent of welfare expenditure to families in 1979 but cornering 46 per cent less than 20 years later) holds in part the genesis of today's welfare dependency. Changes to the job base have also, of course, to be included here. In counter position to the orthodox anti-poverty strategy, *Making Welfare Work* advocated an insurance base where universalism takes clear priority over the level of benefit, where this form of benefit encourages additional self- or family-provision, and where the largest dead weight budget, that of income support, is converted into an education and training programme.

Alan Deacon's criticisms are of a different order. Part of his own recent contributions to this area have been in mapping both the direction and the nature of changes in the current social policy debate, and his essay is part of this much larger consignment. There are four aspects of his contribution on which I would like to comment, in addition to the role of human nature to which I have already alluded.

He sees a 'central difficulty' stemming from the interchangeability I have ascribed to the terms character, behaviour and human nature. Specifically he suggests, I confuse behaviour and character in an unnecessarily provocative manner. It was not my intention to use these three terms interchangeably. It was rather my wish to stress that they are distinct but linked. The starting point was that of human nature which had already been described. Character was presented as the sum of values we hold, while behaviour was determined by how our character reacts to events. So my use of the word character was anything but accidental. It was a recognition, rather, that the shaping of certain types of character traits was a proper goal for public policy. Specifically, it is in the public interest to see certain aspects of character develop for their own sake, i.e. the wish to understand and to appreciate our past, for thereby participants may, amongst other things, acquire a degree of civility, as well as character traits which, when responding to events, lead to behaviour which is generally approved—for example, courtesy.

The term character clearly irks Deacon. It reminds him too much of the distinction the Charity Organisation Society (COS) and their cohorts made between the character worthy of help and those cast beyond the pale. I too make a distinction which I thought, from his other writings, was one to which Deacon subscribed. One of welfare's roles is to reward and to punish. The distribution of welfare is one of the great teaching forces open to advanced societies. As Christian morality becomes unsustainable without being recharged in each generation by waves of new Christian believers, so societies must seek different ways of affirming right and wrong conduct. Welfare has such a role. But here the selection for reward or punishment is self-selection (i.e. I am willing or not willing to agree to the conditions attached to benefit) rather than being imposed on the basis of third party personal judgements as, it is alleged, was done by COS workers. This, of course, does not explain why I believe character is being revived in the debate on restructuring welfare. I have nothing to add here because I do not believe character, as I have defined it, should ever have been eclipsed.

Why have I said too little about the limits on individual explanations of poverty? Again, the answer is quite simple. As there is still a galaxy of commentators on the centre-left whose hidden assumption is that poverty is caused by the system (capitalism, racism, sexism, etc.) I have no wish to blunt that part of my argument of which people on the centre-left are still often loath to confront. I did not here stress my belief that Reich's thesis on job creation (investment in people is everything), while generally correct, will not in all particulars offer job opportunities to all those seeking or wishing to work (two different stances again stemming from different character traits and how those characters react to their unemployment). That is an Alcock criticism. What I have to say about the need for a reserve labour market was set out in *Europe Isn't Working* and *Beyond Punishment*.[1]

Deacon is right that I say too little about the premises (and he could have added the form) of a stakeholders' society. The form of the stakeholder institution will be developed in a third volume of these reports (the second volume to *Making Welfare Work* will be *How to Pay For The Future*.) But why a stakeholder society in the first place? My use of the term was not related to its use on the economic front. The use of stakeholding in welfare is simply the result of listening to Will Hutton talk about economic stakeholding during sessions of the Dahrendorf Commission and thinking that this phrase could be the *leitmotif* of a whole government programme, and particularly as it related to welfare reform.

The genesis of the idea of stakeholding welfare was nothing more than this. Its attraction was that it met the needs of the hour: how to gain approval for increasing welfare expenditure at a time when all the effective pressures are targeted at the opposite objective, and in favour of direct tax cuts. Only by changing the rules, i.e. to collective provision which is individually owned, was it possible to square this particular circle. And, as personal ownership of pensions capital and the ownership insurance scheme were necessary changes, stakeholding seemed to me to signify the magnitude of the changes which were being proposed.

What has yet to be spelt out is how stakeholding welfare changes fundamentally what is meant by one important aspect of citizenship. Just as stakeholding can be used as a phrase covering a multitude of different thoughts, or none, so, as T. H. Marshall was the first to conceptualise, citizenship has been developed and enhanced by the universalisation of welfare provision in the post-war period. It can of course be argued that the monumental switch to means testing has, in effect, undermined any reality of equal citizenship which welfare promoted. Even so, by changing the balance of welfare so decisively again—this time towards stakeholding — full citizenship, as comprehended by many people, will be redefined. As stakeholding will become a new badge of citizenship, non-stakeholding will become an agent of exclusion. Hence the importance I have attached to the extension of stakeholding status to those who by chance (not choice) are outside a labour market through which stakeholding is acquired.

David Green's many criticisms would be correct if his interpretation of the Stakeholder Corporations was sound. Their existence (one to cover pension universalisation and another to run a new national insurance scheme) is not a surreptitious attempt to recoup for the state what is clearly slipping beyond its grasp. For someone who advocated council house sales back in 1976, and the use of the released capital to repair and rebuild, I have not gone native and devised new means of maintaining the state-imposed serfdom I then attacked. The stakeholding organisations are a genuine attempt to help rebuild the very civic culture for which Green has so powerfully called.

Another matter of substance is Green's assertion that 'our capacity to adopt moral virtues as our own cannot be satisfactorily understood with the language of incentives'. I could not agree more. Although, as I have explained earlier, I might have phrased that as virtuous behaviour or even character, not moral virtue. While Green appears to see virtue being acquired through osmosis (and it clearly is as people absorb the norms and values around them) so I believe that welfare incentives are too important a force not to be acknowledged now as a primary influence. The proportions were given earlier. Very nearly half of today's welfare bill going to those below retirement age is means-tested, and, as I believe more strongly than apparently than does the IEA spokesman, men and women are rational economic creatures (though not exclusively so). The £31 billion spent on means-tested welfare for one in three of the population is shaping a response (behaviour) more directly, and impacting in a more deadly manner, than osmosis can ever do.

The criticisms made by Melanie Phillips are ones to which I have the least complete answer. I seek to tackle poverty amongst single parents. Phillips retorts that 'the main problem with lone motherhood is not poverty but the fact that it is an undesirable state in which to bring up children. Working is an antidote to unemployment; but motherhood is not unemployment'. Phillips dispassionately argues that the skills necessary to juggle working and motherhood are beyond most single never-married mothers.

I am anxious not to open up new swathes of debate in this rejoinder. But the meaning of never-married single motherhood has changed in my lifetime, not merely in numbers but in its very nature. Never-married mothers are often as not not single in the generally accepted meaning of that term. Lack of high-paying unskilled work poses for many young males a major disincentive to marriage as opposed to sub-letting their own flat on which the rent has been fully covered by housing benefit, drawing income support as a single person, and living with their girlfriend. There are in reality often two parents although only one parent ever appears in the official statistics.

I am conscious that this paragraph does grave injustice to the complexity of the living arrangements which single people and partners arrange. I merely pose it to suggest that Phillips' model is not a universal one, even for the never-married mothers. So what I say requiring all working age claimants to draw up life objectives, and use income support to try and achieve the first part of this journey, has some relevance, although it is clearly no universal panacea. Expressed simply, many of those single never-married mothers will be responding to the new welfare framework from a basis where they are living full-time with a partner. Similarly, I have no wish to underestimate what virtuous behaviour will be unlocked once the prohibitive restrictions imposed by welfare rules on its blooming have been removed.

There is, however, another key dilemma. All too many of today's political leaders were active supporters of a relativist code of conduct which refused to rank human behaviour. It is safer to preach and act such a line of course if daddy has a big bank balance to full back upon. But at a time when the financial advantages of marriage have lessened, when jobs paying family wages are on the decline, priorities about childrearing have come under attack. This left the poorest and least able bearing the full brunt of this particular vicious era of political correctness that single parenthood is equal, if not superior, to two-parent families as a unit in which to raise children.

I am loath to blame the victim. What is required are policies which help single mothers to do the very best they can in raising their children, while at the same time attempting to cut the supply route to unmarried single parenthood. At any time such a dual approach would be difficult. It is doubly so in an age where sound bites reign supreme. It nevertheless has to be attempted. So, while I have no certain answer nor, sadly, does Phillips.

Notes

1 Field, F., *Europe Isn't Working*, London: Institute of Community Studies, 1994; and Field, F. and Owen, M., *Beyond Punishment: Hard Choices on the Road to Full Employability*, London: Institute of Community Studies, 1995.

How To Pay For The £uture:

Building a Stakeholders' Welfare

Frank Field

Including costings by the Government Actuary's Department

How To Pay For The £uture develops the strategy for reconstructing Britain's welfare system first outlined in **Making Welfare Work**. The second of a three volume series, this book;

■ extends the argument that means-tested benefit penalises self-help and discourages self-improvement while taxing honesty and saving;

■ explains how means-tested benefit rewards claimants for being inactive and deceitful;

■ advances welfare reforms which reflect both self-interest and altruism.

How To Pay For The £uture contains detailed proposals for building a genuine stakeholders' welfare system. The programme comprises:

■ universal contributions towards second pensions, with clearly ascribed ownership rights for each stakeholder;

■ a new national stakeholder insurance system which ties benefits to contributions;

■ a proactive income support agency which helps claimants build their own exits from welfare dependency.

How To Pay For The £uture argues that universal welfare provision can only be guaranteed by combining individual contributions to savings and insurance schemes with stakeholder ownership and control.

How To Pay For The £uture includes costings from the Government Actuary's Department.

Frank Field is Member of Parliament for Birkenhead and Chairman of the Social Security Select Committee.

How To Pay for the Future:
Building a Stakeholder's Welfare

Frank Field

The cost of each copy is £40 for institutions and companies and £10 for individuals.

Please make cheques payable to:

The Institute of Community Studies

Name..

Company...

Address..

....

....

....

Please return this form to:

The Institute of Community Studies
18 Victoria Park Square
London E2 9PF